GUIDELINES FOR CLIMATE-RESILIENT, GENDER-RESPONSIVE, AND SOCIALLY INCLUSIVE PUBLIC OPEN SPACES IN BANGLADESH

JULY 2024

ASIAN DEVELOPMENT BANK

 Creative Commons Attribution 3.0 IGO license (CC BY 3.0 IGO)

© 2024 Asian Development Bank
6 ADB Avenue, Mandaluyong City, 1550 Metro Manila, Philippines
Tel +63 2 8632 4444; Fax +63 2 8636 2444
www.adb.org

Some rights reserved. Published in 2024.

ISBN 978-92-9270-785-9 (print); 978-92-9270-786-6 (PDF); 978-92-9270-787-3 (e-book)
Publication Stock No. TIM240341-2
DOI: http://dx.doi.org/10.22617/TIM240341-2

The views expressed in this publication are those of the authors and do not necessarily reflect the views and policies of the Asian Development Bank (ADB) or its Board of Governors or the governments they represent.

ADB does not guarantee the accuracy of the data included in this publication and accepts no responsibility for any consequence of their use. The mention of specific companies or products of manufacturers does not imply that they are endorsed or recommended by ADB in preference to others of a similar nature that are not mentioned.

By making any designation of or reference to a particular territory or geographic area in this document, ADB does not intend to make any judgments as to the legal or other status of any territory or area.

This work is available under the Creative Commons Attribution 3.0 IGO license (CC BY 3.0 IGO) https://creativecommons.org/licenses/by/3.0/igo/. By using the content of this publication, you agree to be bound by the terms of this license. For attribution, translations, adaptations, and permissions, please read the provisions and terms of use at https://www.adb.org/terms-use#openaccess.

This CC license does not apply to non-ADB copyright materials in this publication. If the material is attributed to another source, please contact the copyright owner or publisher of that source for permission to reproduce it. ADB cannot be held liable for any claims that arise as a result of your use of the material.

Please contact pubsmarketing@adb.org if you have questions or comments with respect to content, or if you wish to obtain copyright permission for your intended use that does not fall within these terms, or for permission to use the ADB logo.

Corrigenda to ADB publications may be found at http://www.adb.org/publications/corrigenda.

Note:
In this publication, "$" refers to United States dollars.

On the cover: People wait on the platform at the Kamlapur Railway Station in Dhaka (photo by Abir Abdullah).

Contents

Tables, Figures, and Boxes	v
Foreword	vii
Message	ix
Acknowledgments	x
Abbreviations	xii
Glossary	xiii

Introduction   1
    Background and Objectives   1

Prioritize and Prepare   5
    1.1 Constitute a Preliminary Team   5
    1.2 Prioritize and Select a Public Open Space   5
    1.3 Assess and Strengthen the Capacity of the *Pourashava*   7
    1.4 Prepare a Communications and Outreach Strategy   8
    1.5 Prepare a Base Map and Conduct a Reconnaissance Survey   10

Assess   12
    2.1 Assess the Local Blue Green–Gray Network and the Impact of Climate Risks on the Public Open Space   12
    2.2 Conduct a Detailed Assessment of the Public Open Space   14
    2.3 Conduct Participatory Safety Audits   20
    2.4 Conduct Participatory Accessibility Audits   20
    2.5 Understand the Barriers and Expectations of Diverse Groups   21

Create   24
    3.1 Facilitate a Multistakeholder Visioning Workshop   24
    3.2 Create a Concept Plan   24
    3.3 Test On-Site and Obtain Feedback   36

Implement   39
    4.1 Prepare the Project Proposal   39
    4.2 Plan the Implementation Modality   39
    4.3 Prepare the Tender Documents   40
    4.4 Manage Construction Activities   40

Manage — **42**
    5.1 Identify Maintenance Funding Sources — 42
    5.2 Develop an Operation and Maintenance Plan — 42
    5.3 Create a Monitoring and Evaluation Plan — 44

Conclusion — **46**

Appendixes — **48**
    1 Prepare and Prioritize — 51
    2 Assess — 57
    3 Create — 71
    4 Manage — 85

References — **87**

Tables, Figures, and Boxes

Tables

1	Criteria for Comparative Assessment of Public Open Spaces	6
2	Illustrative Communication Tools	8
3	Stages, Outputs, and Indicative Communication Methods at Each Project Stage	9
4	Assessments for Various Hazards at the Metropolitan Region, Precinct, and Site Scales	13
5	Objectives and Strategies to Strengthen Climate Adaptation	26
6	Design Criteria for Different Age Groups	30
7	Implementation Schedule for 1-Week-Long Pilot Testing	37
8	Indicators to Assess Impact of the Trial	37
9	Implementation Modalities and Characteristics	39
10	Elements of a Maintenance Model	42
11	Different Models for Maintenance of Public Open Spaces in Bangladesh	43
A3.1	Proposed Amenity Hubs at Different Locations	80
A3.2	Design Elements for Rupa Chaudhary Pouro Park	82

Figures

1	Types of Public Open Spaces	2
2	Guiding Principles	2
3	Creating and Maintaining Climate-Resilient, Gender-Responsive, and Socially Inclusive Public Open Spaces	3
4	Selecting a Public Open Space	5
5	Stakeholder Mapping Based on Affinity and Influence	6
6	Degrees of Public Participation	8
7	Indicative Communication Methods at Each Project Stage	9
8	Example of a Base Map of a Public Open Space	10
9	An Illustration of Slope Analysis for Barishal–Pathuakali Road, Kuakata	12
10	An Illustration of Assessing Connectivity and Access	15
11	An Illustration of Mapping Building Usage	16
12	An Illustration of Gender Counts at Different Times of Day	16
13	An Illustration of Assessing Climate Adaptation Interventions	17
14	An Illustration of Assessing Safety and Security	18
15	An Illustration of Mapping the Street Furniture and Amenities	18
16	Creating a Local Water Management Network Plan	25
17	Trees and Shrubs for Coastal Towns	28
18	An Illustration for Improving Connectivity and Accessibility	29
19	An Illustration of a Concept Plan	31
20	Before and After Rendering of a Pathway in Rupa Chaudhary Pouro Park	31
21	Improving Safety and Security	32
22	Nursing Room	33
23	Framework for Designing Gender-Responsive Public Toilet	34
24	Allocating Space for Street Vendors	34
25	Using Material Suitable for All-Weather Conditions	35

26	Barisal–Patuakhali Road in Kuakata	35
27	Tactical Trial at Sector 2 Market, Rohtak	36
28	Concept Design of a Pedestrianized Street in Kuakata	37
29	Continuous Walkway Along the Lake Edge in Jessore Pouro Park	44
A3.1	Connectivity and Access Roads to Kuakata	76
A3.2	Concrete Embankment Installed Along Kuakata Beach to Combat Rising Tides	76
A3.3	Stakeholder Consultation Process	77
A3.4	Visioning Workshop with the Community in Kuakata	77
A3.5	Guiding Principles	77
A3.6	Proposed Concept Strategies along the Road	78
A3.7	Detailed Street Sections	78
A3.8	Concept Design Near Booking Counters	79
A3.9	Concept Design of a Pedestrianized Street	79
A3.10	National Helpline Numbers	80
A3.11	Map of Rupa Chaudhary Pouro Park	81
A3.12	Stakeholder Consultation Process	82
A3.13	Guiding Principles	82
A3.14	Concept Plan	83
A3.15	National Helpline Numbers	84

Boxes

1	Consider Constituting a Public Open Space Working Group	7
2	Ethical Considerations	22

Foreword

The Asian Development Bank (ADB) is committed to making cities more livable. This is one of ADB's seven operational priorities under Strategy 2030. Over the last 2 decades, ADB has supported the Government of Bangladesh in its holistic development of sustainable urban centers, specifically in strengthening urban planning and fostering gender-responsive, inclusive, and participatory processes and environments.

ADB was pleased to support the Local Government Engineering Department (LGED) in its preparation of the *Guidelines for Climate-Resilient and Gender and Socially Inclusive Public Open Spaces in Cities and Towns in Bangladesh*. With its ambitious mandate from the outset, the guidelines outline a participatory process and provides tools to achieve three key goals: climate adaptation, gender equality, and social inclusion in public open space selection, design, implementation, and management. The guidelines' development followed an innovative iterative process, as it was tested in the cities of Bagerhat and Kuakata and learned from ongoing good practices in public open space design in Bangladesh.

Gender-responsive and inclusive public space design in cities contributes toward three of the Sustainable Development Goals (SDGs): SDG 5 on achieving gender equality and empowering women and girls; SDG 11 on making cities and human settlements inclusive, safe, resilient, and sustainable; and SDG 16 on promoting peaceful and inclusive societies for sustainable development. The guidelines will support *pourashavas* and the LGED to localize SDGs at the city level.

These guidelines were developed as a part of the Coastal Towns Climate Resilience Project and is a collaboration of two ADB regional knowledge support technical assistance (TA) projects—TA 6737: Advancing the Transformative Gender Equality Agenda in a Post-COVID-19 Asia and the Pacific and TA 9919: Integrated and Innovative Solutions for More Livable Cities.

Gender-responsive and inclusive planning and design help women, girls, gender minorities, and people with disabilities to feel safe in the city and enable them to carry out their daily activities and enjoy its amenities. It also purposefully creates a city that is friendly to children and older people. I hope the insights that this publication offers will provide cross-regional learning to foster innovative urban development across Asia and the Pacific, to meet the evolving needs and interests of all.

Bruno Carrasco
Director General
Climate Change and Sustainable Development Department
Asian Development Bank

Foreword

The Local Government Engineering Department (LGED) has been contributing toward the national economic and social development of Bangladesh through its rural and urban infrastructure development efforts. Due to the increasing urbanization rate in Bangladesh, densification in urban areas, and the coronavirus disease (COVID-19) pandemic, the need for quality public open spaces has been felt more than ever before. Therefore, the LGED is increasingly involved in public open space development along with other urban infrastructure and services subprojects.

While our master plans provide for new public open spaces, there is an opportunity to redesign urban roads, underutilized government lands, and organically developed public open spaces. There are numerous good practice examples of public open spaces in Bangladesh. However, there is a need for guidelines to consolidate the learnings, outline a process, and provide tools that can be consistently applied across cities and towns in Bangladesh. Public open spaces can aid in climate adaptation and enable access for all, especially women, girls, gender minorities, and people with disabilities.

The Asian Development Bank has developed climate-resilient and gender and socially inclusive public open space design guidelines for urban areas in Bangladesh, with a focus on coastal towns. The LGED has adopted these guidelines as it will be relevant for all urban areas in Bangladesh, especially secondary and small towns. The guidelines are aligned with Sustainable Development Goal 11 and New Urban Agenda commitments of the 8th Five-Year Plan, the Delta Plan 2100, the National Adaptation Plan, the Persons with Disabilities Rights and Protection Act in 2013, the National Women Development Policy 2011, and the Gender Strategy and Action Plan of the LGED. These guidelines outline participatory processes and tools to select, design, implement, and manage public open spaces.

We will scale up these guidelines at the national level. I believe these guidelines will help the LGED, local urban governments, and other stakeholders deliver the best outcomes for public open spaces in Bangladesh. Finally, I express my heartfelt thanks and congratulations to those who were involved in the formulation of these guidelines.

Sheikh Muhammad Mohsin
Chief Engineer
Local Government Engineering Department

Message

2023 marks 50 years of partnership between Bangladesh and the Asian Development Bank (ADB). Since Bangladesh became a member of ADB in 1973, ADB had provided $29.71 billion in 834 projects by April 2023 and the partnership has extended to almost all areas of the country. In the urban sector, ADB has been working with Bangladesh to improve infrastructure, enhance services delivery, and strengthen urban governance to make cities more livable.

This *Guidelines for Climate-Resilient and Gender and Socially Inclusive Public Open Spaces for Cities and Towns in Bangladesh* comes in times of need. For ADB's urban operations, these guidelines strengthen our transformation from sector-based investments to an integrated urban development approach that is climate-adaptive, gender and socially inclusive, and people-centric. Such a transformation will continue contributing to Bangladesh's endeavor to improve climate and disaster resilience. As Bangladesh continues to urbanize rapidly, I believe these guidelines offer demand-shaping opportunities for designing public open spaces that are accessible and beneficial to all residents.

ADB initiated the work of these guidelines in 2021 to support the Bangladesh Coastal Towns Climate Resilience Project. We wanted these guidelines to support 22 selected coastal *pourashavas* in pursuing sustainable development and enhancing the quality of life of their residents. To scale up the impact, ADB then applied these guidelines to our proposed results-based loan for the Bangladesh: Improving Urban Governance and Infrastructure Program, which will support 88 *pourashavas* in achieving integrated and sustainable urban development to improve their livability. Today, I am glad to see that these guidelines are well received by the Local Government Engineering Department, and that it will be distributed widely to guide the development of climate-resilient and gender and socially inclusive public open spaces across Bangladesh.

I commend the team for their efforts in producing these guidelines. I am confident that these guidelines will inspire urban planners, engineers, architects, as well as ADB project officers and other development partners to create more quality public open spaces in Bangladesh cities and towns and beyond.

Samantha Hung
Director
Gender Equality Division
Climate Change and Sustainable Development Department
Asian Development Bank

Norio Saito
Senior Director
Water and Urban Development Sector Office
Sectors Group
Asian Development Bank

Acknowledgments

The *Guidelines for Climate-Resilient and Gender and Socially Inclusive Public Open Spaces in Cities and Towns of Bangladesh* is a collaborative effort between the Local Government Engineering Department (LGED) and the two regional knowledge sharing technical assistance (TA) programs within the Asian Development Bank (ADB)—TA 6737: Advancing the Transformative Gender Equality Agenda in a Post-COVID-19 Asia and the Pacific and TA 9919: Integrated and Innovative Solutions for More Livable Cities. It contributes to the work under ADB's Bangladesh: Coastal Towns Climate Resilience Project (CTCRP).

The team is grateful to Samantha Hung, Director, Gender Equality Division and Manoj Sharma, Director, Water and Urban Development Sector Office for their guidance and support in the preparation of this publication.

These guidelines were prepared by:

The ADB Team:
Laxmi Sharma, Senior Urban Development Specialist, Water and Urban Development Sector Office (SG-WUD), Sectors Group (SG); Prabhjot Khan, Social Development Specialist (Gender and Development), Gender Equality Division (CCGE), Climate Change and Sustainable Development Department; Sunghoon Kris Moon, Urban Development Specialist, SG-WUD, SG; SA Abdullah Mamun, Senior Project Officer (Urban Infrastructure), Bangladesh Resident Mission; Saswati Belliappa, Senior Safeguards Specialist, Office of Safeguards; Sarah Hui Li, Urban Development Specialist (Consultant), SG-WUD, SG; Ian Munt, Urban Development Specialist (Consultant), SG-WUD, SG

The Guidelines Design Consultant Team:
Core team members: Sonal Shah, Gender and Urban Planning Expert (Team Leader); Muhammad Shamsuzzaman, Urban Design Expert; Masreka Khan, Gender and Community Engagement Expert; Apoorv Garg, Urban Design Expert

Supporting team members: Muhammad Habib Ullah, Community Engagement Assistant; Muhammad Tamzid, Assistant Urban Designer; Nasir Uddin Sheikh, Translator; Nazmus Sadat, Interpreter; Rhea Marie Francisco, Technical Assistance Coordinator (Consultant), CCGE; Shradha Gupta, Urban Designer and Visual Assistant

LGED:
Sheikh Muhammad Mohsin, Chief Engineer; AKM Rezaul Islam, Project Director, Urban Governance infrastructure Improvement Project-3; Muhammad Nazrul Islam, former Project Director of CTCRP

Pourashavas:
Anwar Hossain Hawladar, Mayor of Kuakata Pourashava; Khan Habibur Rahman, Mayor of Bagerhat Pourashava; Abul Hossain, Sub-Assistant Engineer, Kuakata Pourashava; SM Sharif Hossain (Executive Engineer), Sikder Moklachur Rahman andBM Kamal Ahmed (Assistant Engineers), Sultana Sajia (Town Planner); Jessore Pourashava; TM Rezaul Rizvi, Assistant Engineer, Bagerhat Pourashava

Acknowledgments

The team wishes to thank the following for **sharing their knowledge on good practices in public open space design in Bangladesh**: Professor Enamul Kabir, Forestry and Wood Technology Discipline, Khulna University; Khondaker Hasibul Kabir and his team from CoCreation Architects; Professor Zakiul Islam, Head of the Department of Architecture and his team from Bangladesh University of Engineering and Technology; Ziaur Rahman, Naima Akter, and Gaous Pearee from Work for Better Bangladesh.

We appreciate the support of **civil society organizations** in participating in online consultations and collaborating with us in participatory audits, design charrettes, visioning workshops, and validation workshops:

Muhammad Allama Iqbal Ahmed, Action on Disability and Development International, Kuakata; Chan Chan, Shiri, Kuakata; Chan Chan Oen, Jema Oen, Mili Akter, Latachapli primary school, Kuakata; Chao and Ushi, Rakhain Market Shop Owners Association in Kuakata; Muhammad Firooz, Mst Nasreen, Shankalpo, Bagerhat; Payel Chandra Das, World Concern; Late Muhammad Shahiduzzaman, Amena Begum, Voice of South.

We appreciate the **valuable and extensive peer review** from the following experts:

Amit Datta Roy, Senior Project Officer (Infrastructure), Bangladesh Resident Mission, ADB; Bai Jie, Urban Development Specialist, SG-WUD, ADB; Charlene Liau, Urban Development Specialist, SG-WUD, ADB; Christian Walder, Urban Development Specialist, ADB; Chris Zevenbergen, Professor, IHE Delft Institute for Water Education; Haidy Ear-Dupuy, Unit Head, NGO and Civil Society Center, Fragility and Engagement Division, ADB; Iain McKinnon, Co-founder and Director, Global Disability Innovation Hub, University College London; Iftekhar Ahmed, Programme Advisor, United Nations Office for Project Services (Bangladesh); Jaemin Nam, Senior Urban Development Specialist, SG-WUD, ADB; Ma. Victoria Antonio, Monitoring and Evaluation Specialist (Consultant), Urban Climate Change and Resilience Trust Fund, ADB; Naresh Giri, Senior Project Officer (Urban Development), Nepal Resident Mission, ADB; Nasheeba Selim, Senior Social Development Officer (Gender), Bangladesh Resident Mission, ADB; Sanjay Joshi, Principal Urban Development Specialist, SG-WUD, ADB; Uzma Altaf, Gender Specialist, CCGE, ADB.

Last but not least, we are grateful to around 150 people who participated in the safety audits, accessibility audits, visioning workshops, exhibitions, and validation workshops.

Abbreviations

ADB	Asian Development Bank
GBV	gender-based violence
GIS	geographic information system
LGED	Local Government Engineering Department
SDG	Sustainable Development Goal
SEAH	sexual exploitation, abuse, and harassment
TLCC	Town-Level Coordination Committee
UN-Habitat	United Nations Human Settlement Programme
UNICEF	United Nations Children's Fund
WLCC	Ward-Level Coordination Committee

Glossary

Accessibility audits assess what barriers may exist that reduce access and participation of people with disabilities, and what measures can be taken to eliminate these barriers (UN Women 2021).

Adolescents include individuals in the age groups of 10–19 years.

Bazaars are markets (as in the Middle East) consisting of rows of shops or stalls selling miscellaneous goods (Merriam-Webster n.d.).

Beach erosion is the carrying away of beach materials by wave action, tidal currents, littoral currents, or wind (USACE 2003).

Bioswales are a green infrastructure which reduce runoff velocity and cleanse water while recharging the underlying groundwater table (NACTO 2013).

Blue-green-gray network combines ecosystem conservation and/or restoration with the selective use of conventional engineering approaches to provide solutions that deliver climate change resilience and adaptation benefits. By blending "green" conservation with "gray" engineering techniques, communities can incorporate the benefits of both solutions (Conservation International 2019).

Breakwaters is an offshore coastal defense structure built of stone, parallel to the coastline. It helps absorb the energy of breaking waves. Deposition occurs in the calmer water created behind the breakwater (Barcelona Field Studies Centre S.L. n.d.). It protects a shore area, harbor, anchorage, or basin from waves (USACE 2003).

Climate adaptation ameliorates the impact of climate risks on communities and strengthens their resilience. In human systems, adaptation seeks to moderate harm or use beneficial opportunities. In natural systems, human intervention may facilitate adjustment to the expected climate and its effects (MoEFCC 2022).

Climate resilience is the capacity of a socio-ecological system to cope with a hazardous climate event, responding or reorganizing in ways that maintain its essential function, identity, and structure while also maintaining the capacity for adaptation, learning, and transformation (MoEFCC 2022).

Climate vulnerability is the degree to which a system is susceptible to and unable to cope with the adverse effects of climate change, including climate variability and extremes. Vulnerability is a function of the character, magnitude, and rate of climate change, and the variation to which a system is exposed, its sensitivity, and its adaptive capacity (MoEFCC 2022).

Coastal floods occur due to tidal or storm-driven coastal events, including storm surges in lower coastal waterways. This can be exacerbated by wind-wave generation from storm events (Queensland Reconstruction Authority 2011–2022).

Dedicated pathways are pedestrian paths, bicycle paths, or other areas for use by people, but not by motor vehicles (State Government of Victoria 2016).

Design charrette is an intensive, hands-on workshop that brings people from different disciplines and backgrounds together with members of the community to explore design options for a particular area (Involve 2018).

Extreme heat is defined as summertime temperatures that are much hotter and/or more humid than average. Because some places are hotter than others, this depends on what is considered average for a particular location at that time of year (CDCP 2017).

Focus group discussions are guided discussions of a small group of people. They are normally one-off sessions although several may be run simultaneously in different locations. The group needs to be small (6–12 people) for participants to feel comfortable voicing their views. Members of the focus group can be selected to be demographically representative or of a specific subset of the population (Involve 2018).

Gender refers to the socially constructed roles, attributes, and opportunities associated with being male and female (WHO 2011).

Gender-based violence (GBV) refers to any type of harm that is perpetrated against a person or group of people because of their biological or perceived sex, gender, sexual orientation, and/or gender identity. Gender-based violence can be sexual, physical, verbal, psychological (emotional), or socioeconomic, and it can take many forms (Council of Europe 2023).

Gender equality means that men and women have the opportunity to develop their full potential and make their own choices free from the limitations set by stereotypes, gender roles, or prejudices. It does not mean that men and women must become the same, but that their rights, responsibilities, and opportunities will not depend on whether they are born male or female. It means men and women have equal (i) rights under customary or statutory law; (ii) opportunities and access to resources to enhance their human capabilities, productivity, and earnings; and (iii) voice to influence and contribute to the decision-making in governing structures, institutions, and the development process in their communities (ADB, Guidelines for Gender Mainstreaming Categories of ADB Projects 2021).

Gender minorities are individuals whose gender identity (man, woman, other) or expression (masculine, feminine, other) is different from their sex (male, female) assigned at birth (CDCP 2022).

Gender norms are the informal rules and shared beliefs that distinguish expected behavior based on gender identities at particular points in time and social contexts. They are usually internalized during childhood and adolescence and continue to shape gender stereotyping throughout the life course (UNICEF 2020).

Gender-responsive approaches includes specific action to reduce gender inequalities within communities (UNFPA and UNICEF 2021).

Gender roles are the expected roles, including behaviors, activities, and responsibilities, associated with each sex (UNICEF 2020).

Gender-sensitive approaches recognize different needs of men, women, boys, and girls, and acknowledges gender power dynamics, but does not necessarily address these other than to try and integrate an understanding of these dynamics (UNFPA and UNICEF 2021).

Gender socialization refers to processes by which individuals (especially children and adolescents) internalize gender norms. Internalization refers to a process of learning what norms are, understanding why they are of value or make sense, and accepting norms as one's own. Positive gender socialization refers to processes that challenge and change harmful norms to achieve gender-equitable outcomes (UNICEF 2020).

Gravel bed filter prevents dirt and pollutants (such as oil and grease) from entering the stormwater drain and water bodies. It includes multiple layers of sand or gravel (Oasis Design Inc. New Delhi, India 2012).

Groins are narrow, roughly shore-normal structures built to reduce longshore currents, and/or to trap and retain littoral material. Most groins are of timber or rock and extend from a seawall or the backshore, well onto the foreshore (USACE 2003).

Injection wells are used primarily to recharge confined aquifers. The design of an injection well for artificial recharge is like that of a water supply well. The principal difference is that water flows from the injection well into the surrounding aquifer under either a gravity head or a head maintained by an injection pump. The system may be a series of specifically placed injection wells or a combination of injection and pumping wells where water is injected or pumped to form a hydraulic barrier (California Department of Water Resources n.d.).

Key informant interviews are qualitative in-depth interviews with people knowledgeable about a theme, sector, or a community. These include community leaders, decision-makers, professionals, or residents who can provide insight into the nature of problems and give recommendations for solutions (UCLA Center for Health Policy Research 2005).

Khals are drainage channels built around fields to capture freshwater during the annual floods of the wet season. Khals allow farmers to release freshwater into their fields, individual canal sections at a time, to flush out the salt that would otherwise build up in the soil (Chambwera et al. 2011).

Mudflat refers to land near a body of water that is regularly flooded by tides and is usually barren. Also known as tidal flats, mudflats are formed with mud deposits by tides or rivers. Mudflats protect the inland landforms from erosion and act as a barrier to waves from eroding land in the interior portions. Further, sea level rise, triggered by global warming, is submerging significant sections of these mudflats. The loss of these tidal flats will make coastal areas vulnerable to the forces of erosion and floods (CDD 2019).

Multi-hazard means (i) the selection of multiple major hazards that the country faces, and (ii) the specific contexts where hazardous events may occur simultaneously, or cumulatively over time, and considering the potential interrelated effects (UNDRR n.d.).

Nature-based solutions are actions to protect, sustainably manage, and restore natural and modified ecosystems that address societal challenges effectively and adaptively, simultaneously benefiting people and nature (MoEFCC 2022).

One-on-one discussion is a commonly used data collection method in health and social research. The individual interview is a valuable method of gaining insight into people's perceptions, understandings, and experiences of a given phenomenon, and can contribute to in-depth data collection. However, the interview is more than a conversational interaction between two people and requires considerable knowledge and skill on behalf of the interviewer (Frances, Coughlan, and Cronin 2009).

Paratransit forms of transportation services are more flexible and personalized than conventional fixed-route, fixed-schedule services. The vehicles are usually low- or medium-capacity vehicles, and the service offered is adjustable in various degrees to individual users' desires. Its categories are public, which is available to any user who pays a predetermined fare (e.g., autos, share autos), and semipublic, which is available only to people of a certain group, such as older people; employees of a company; or residents of a neighborhood (e.g., vanpools, subscription buses). These services are usually informal and oftentimes fill the gaps in the public transport network (GIZ 2020).

Permeable pavements effectively treat, detain, and infiltrate stormwater runoff where landscape-based strategies are restricted or less desired. Pervious pavements have multiple applications, including sidewalks, street furniture zones, and entire roadways (or just their parking lane or gutter strip portions) (NACTO 2013).

Person with disability is a person whose mobility and capacity to use a building or part thereof or a facility are affected due to one or more physical and/or sensory disabilities or impairments (BNBC 2015).

Placemaking refers to a collaborative process by which the public realm can be shaped to maximize shared value. More than just promoting better urban design, placemaking facilitates creative patterns of use, with particular attention to the physical, cultural, and social identities that define a place and support its ongoing evolution (Projects for Public Spaces 2007, PPS 2016).

Public exhibition is an event at which objects such as paintings or photographs are shown to the public, a situation in which someone shows a particular skill or quality to the public (Cambridge Dictionary 2023).

Reconnaissance survey is a preliminary survey, usually executed rapidly and at low cost; a "windshield" survey (BLM 2003).

Resilience is the ability of a system, community, or society exposed to hazards to resist, absorb, accommodate, adapt to, transform, and recover from the effects of a hazard in a timely and efficient manner, including through the preservation and restoration of its essential basic structures and functions through risk management (UNDRR n.d.).

River floods are caused when consistent rain or snow melt forces a river to exceed capacity (WHO n.d.).

Safety audits involve walking through a physical environment to methodically evaluate safety from the perspective of women, girls, and gender minorities. Safety audits empower women to take part in shaping their environment. Safe places and events promote the inclusion and participation of all people in a community, and help to prevent sexual exploitation, abuse, and harassment and all forms of violence. In the context of an audit, "safety" refers to personal safety—specifically, how safe a person is and how safe they feel in any given environment (ACT 2022).

Seawalls are defined as follows: (i) A structure, often concrete or stone, built along a portion of a coast to prevent erosion and other damage by wave action. Often, it retains earth against its shoreward face. (ii) A structure separating land and water areas to alleviate the risk of flooding by the sea. Generally, shore-parallel, although some reclamation seawalls may include lengths that are normal or oblique to the (original) shoreline (USACE 2003).

Sediment trap is an excavated pond or earthen embankment across a low area or drainage swale. It is like a sediment basin, but smaller in size and often temporary in nature. The trap is designed to retain runoff long enough to allow most sediment to settle out (UNEP, CEP 1994).

Sexual exploitation, abuse, and harassment (SEAH) encompasses the following: (i) Sexual exploitation is an actual or attempted abuse of someone's position of vulnerability, differential power or trust, to obtain sexual favors. It also includes trafficking and prostitution. (ii) Sexual abuse is the actual or threatened physical intrusion of a sexual nature, whether by force or under unequal or coercive conditions. It includes sexual slavery, pornography, child abuse, and sexual assault. (iii) Sexual harassment is any unwelcome conduct of a sexual nature that might reasonably be expected or be perceived to cause offense or humiliation (UNHCR 2023).

Social inclusion is a process by which efforts are made to ensure equal opportunities—that everyone, regardless of their background, can achieve their full potential in life. Such efforts include policies and actions that promote equal access to (public) services, as well as enable citizens' participation in the decision-making processes that affect their lives (United Nations 2010).

Stakeholder is any person, organization, institution, social group, or society at large that has a stake in a particular space (GIZ 2020).

Stormwater network is a network of underground pipes and open channels designed for flood control, which discharges straight to creeks and rivers (Sacramento County n.d.).

Tactical trials are city- and/or citizen-led, quick, and affordable ways to test and demonstrate change in physical environments. It is an approach that is premised on using short-term, low-cost, and scalable interventions to catalyze long-term change (GIZ 2020).

Tidal or storm surge is a rise above normal water level on the open coast due to the action of wind stress on the water's surface. Storm surge resulting from a hurricane also includes that rise in level due to atmospheric pressure reduction, as well as that due to wind stress (USACE 2003).

Tot lots are outdoor play areas, especially for younger children (Merriam-Webster n.d.).

Town halls are meeting used for informing the public of emerging or ongoing issues, gauging a community's views of a topic, and identifying solutions to a problem (SAMHSA 2014).

Tree trenches, often known as a "vertical rain garden," is a system that consists of piping for water storage, structural soils, and a tree. It manages stormwater runoff and promotes the use of trees in urban areas (MCWD 2019).

Universal accessibility is the provision in a plot, or a building or a facility, or any part thereof that can be approached, entered, and used without assistance, by persons with limited motion (BNBC 2015), visual, hearing, and neurodivergent persons. Universal access and gender-responsive design specifically addresses accommodations for women such as pregnant women, women with children, and women and girls with disabilities.

Vision workshop is a process that gives residents, business owners, local institutions, and other stakeholders the opportunity to express ideas about the future of their community. In the workshop, participants create a community vision, a written statement that reflects the community's goals and priorities and describes how the community should look and feel in years to come. Ideally, the vision shapes and cultivates a sense of public ownership and buy-in for future land-use decisions and regulations in a municipality, county, or region (The Center for Rural Pennsylvania 2010).

Water scarcity refers to the lack of availability of freshwater resources. Water scarcity is a measure of the physical availability of fresh water rather than whether that water is suitable for use. For instance, a region may have abundant water resources (and thus not be considered water-scarce), but have such severe pollution that those supplies are unfit for human or ecological uses (CEO Water Mandate 2014).

(Water) Wave attenuation structure reduces the amplitude of a wave with distance from the origin and decreases water-particle motion with increasing depth (USACE 2003).

Wave velocity is the speed at which an individual wave advances (USACE 2003).

Wildfire is an unplanned fire—including unauthorized human-caused fires—occurring on forest or range lands, burning forest vegetation, grass, brush, scrub, peat lands, or a prescribed fire set under the regulation which spreads beyond the area authorized for burning (British Columbia 2023).

Kuakata Beach. ADB is developing a guideline to provide climate-resilient public open spaces for cities and towns of Bangladesh (photo by Sonal Shah, ADB).

Introduction

Background and Objectives

Public open spaces define the experience of a town or a city. They improve the quality of life for residents (UN-Habitat 2015), particularly the urban poor; increase climate adaptation for regions vulnerable to disasters such as Bangladesh; and support livelihoods.

The National Building Code outlines standards to estimate the requirement for public open spaces in urban areas of Bangladesh. There is a dearth of planned public open spaces in cities and towns in the country. The Master Plan addresses this gap by providing a blueprint for adequate public open spaces in the long term. *Pourashavas* can redesign existing roads, pedestrian pathways, planned organic public open spaces, and underutilized government lands to improve the quality of life for residents.

There is limited guidance on the role of public open spaces in climate adaptation in Bangladesh, and the tools to enable access for all, especially women, girls, gender minorities, and people with disabilities. For example, research from larger cities in Bangladesh indicates that while women may be involved in numerous community activities, they may not use open spaces for leisure (Jabeen 2019). Adolescent girls are less likely than their male peers to use parks due to spatial and social factors (Brown, Khan, and Hung, 2021). Public open spaces are often inaccessible for people with disabilities, despite the Rights of Persons with Disabilities Act (2013) (WDDF 2014).

Designing public open spaces to increase the presence of different groups of women—young and adolescent girls, pregnant women, elderly women, women with disabilities, resource poor women—can make them inclusive for all. Simultaneously, women's participation in the decision-making of public open space development can ensure that the barriers and expectations of different groups of women and girls are heard and incorporated from the inception. Moreover, when communities see women representing them capably, it influences norms and perceptions about them as leaders. Resources are required to encourage participation and provide training and support to help more women understand how governance and budgets work and what their rights and duties are as representatives (Brown, Khan, and Hung 2021).

Objective

Recognizing this need, the Local Government Engineering Department (LGED) has adopted guidelines to create climate-resilient and gender and socially inclusive public open spaces for cities and towns in Bangladesh. These guidelines outline participatory processes to prioritize, design, implement, and maintain public open spaces in coastal towns. It builds on the learnings of emerging good practices in public space design in Bangladesh (photo); the 8th Five-Year Plan (2020–2025) (GED 2020); and the National Adaptation Plan (MoEFCC 2022), and strengthens the sociocultural and livability needs of the Delta Plan 2100 (GED 2020).

Public Open Space Design at Jallarpar Lake, Naryanganj (photo by Muhammad Shamsuzzaman, ADB).

This publication focuses on the following typologies of public open spaces (Figure 1):[1]

(i) Streets, pedestrian and cycle priority, or dedicated pathways and intersections.

(ii) Planned tot lots, pocket parks, parks, playgrounds, and gardens at the neighborhood and city scales (UN-Habitat, 2020 A).

(iii) Organically developed public open spaces around open-air markets or bazaars, water bodies such as rivers, water channels, khals or lakes.

(iv) Open spaces adjacent to public facilities such as tourism, education, religious, social, transit and cultural amenities, and cyclone shelters.

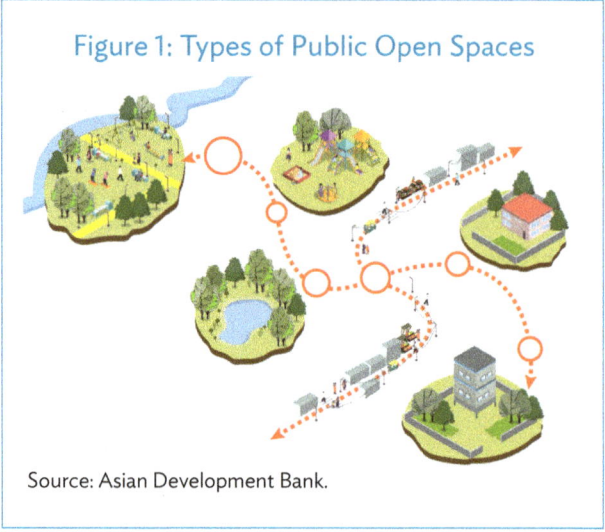

Figure 1: Types of Public Open Spaces

Source: Asian Development Bank.

Primary target audience

The primary target audience are *pourashavas* and the LGED. It will also be a useful resource for advocacy groups, organizations, and consultants working with the *pourashavas*.

Guiding Principles

The process is guided by six interlinked principles (Figure 2).

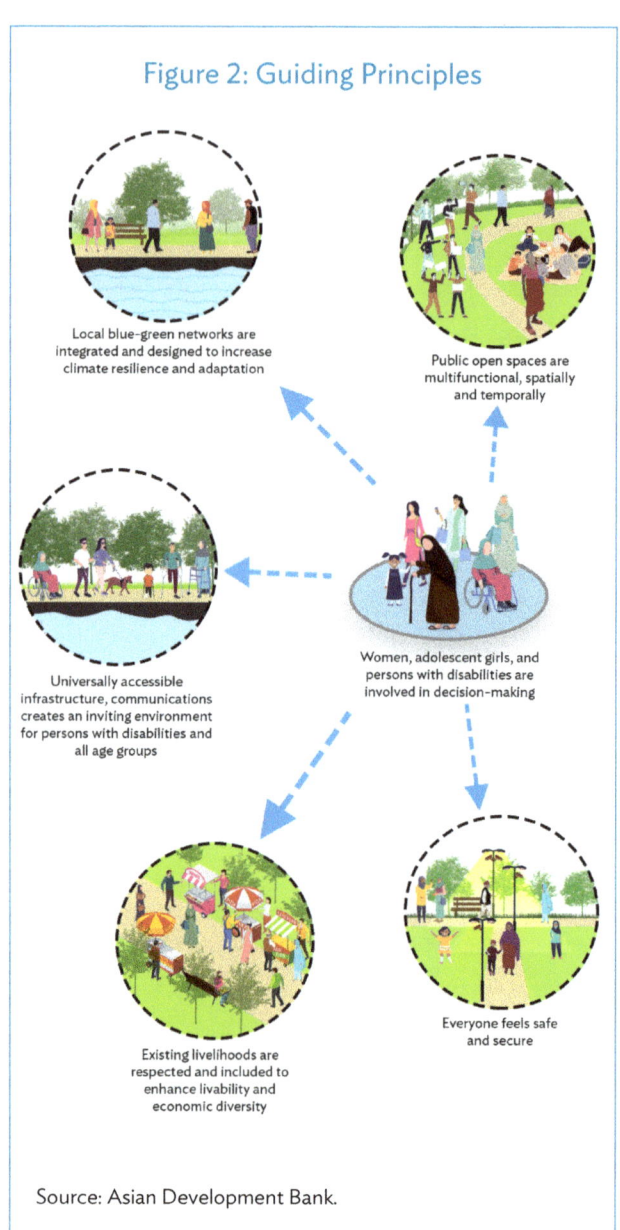

Figure 2: Guiding Principles

- Local blue-green networks are integrated and designed to increase climate resilience and adaptation
- Public open spaces are multifunctional, spatially and temporally
- Universally accessible infrastructure, communications creates an inviting environment for persons with disabilities and all age groups
- Women, adolescent girls, and persons with disabilities are involved in decision-making
- Existing livelihoods are respected and included to enhance livability and economic diversity
- Everyone feels safe and secure

Source: Asian Development Bank.

---

[1] This guideline does not focus on forests, and regional- and national-scale public open spaces such as stadia.

The guidelines are structured as a process and include five stages (Figure 3):

(i) **Prioritize** a public open space and **prepare** by strengthening the *pourashavas* team and creating a communications and engagement strategy.

(ii) **Assess** the public open space using participatory tools.

(iii) **Create** the concept plan, obtain feedback, and test with tactical trials.

(iv) **Implement** the design, identify the modality, obtain approvals from government departments, and prepare contract documents.

(v) **Manage** the public open space, identify a maintenance model, create a management scheme, monitor and evaluate the condition of the public open space regularly.

A checklist outlining the relevant tools for each stage is in Appendix 1-1.

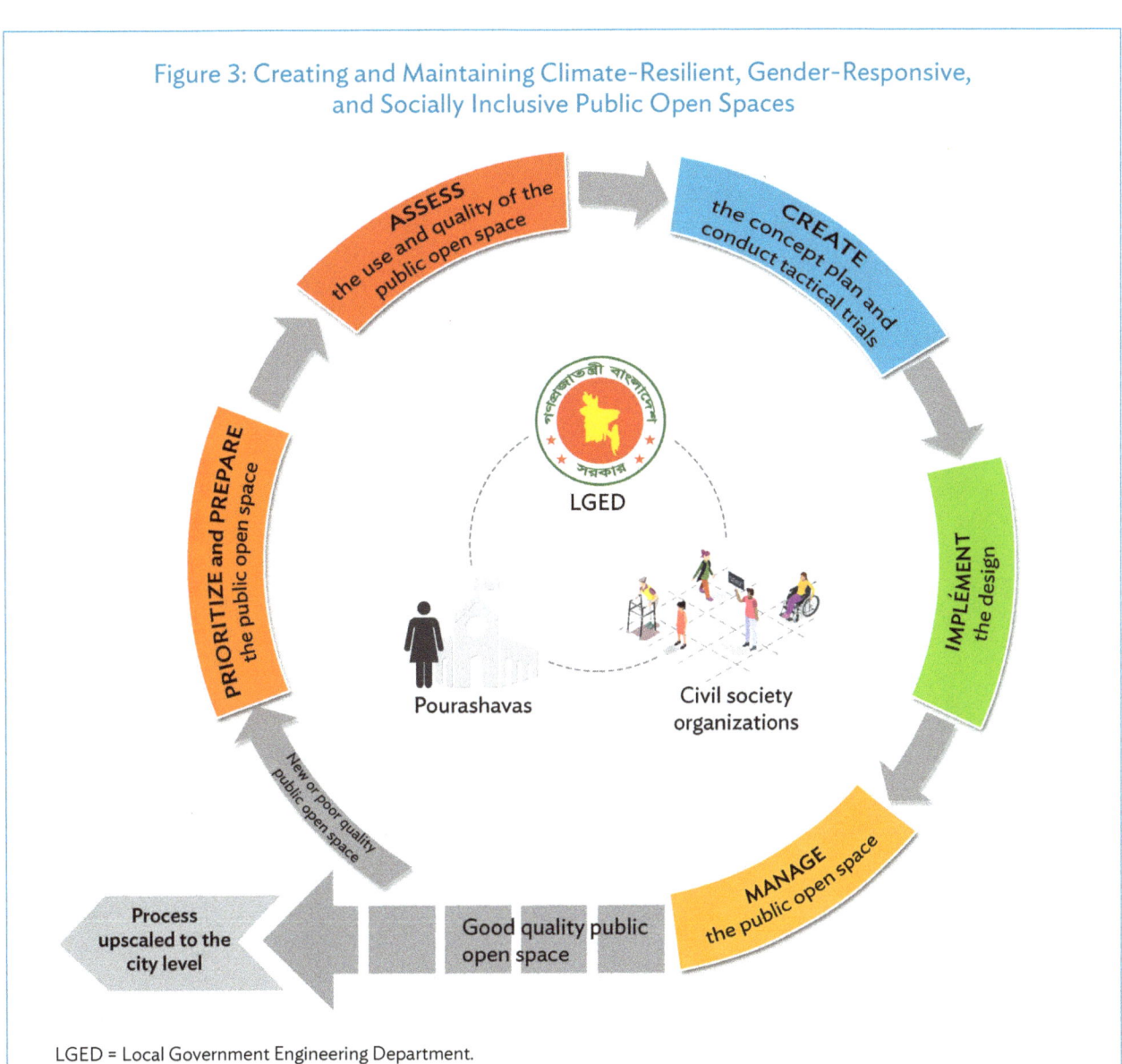

Figure 3: Creating and Maintaining Climate-Resilient, Gender-Responsive, and Socially Inclusive Public Open Spaces

LGED = Local Government Engineering Department.
Source: UN-Habitat. 2020b. *Public Space Site-Specific Assessment: Guidelines to Achieve Quality Public Spaces at Neighbourhood Level*. UN-Habitat.

Shahid Tazuddin Smriti Park at Guishan Avenue, Dhaka. This public open space was designed after collecting expectations from users, particularly from children, and with eco-sensitive design features (photo by Zakiul Islam).

Prioritize and Prepare

1.1 Constitute a Preliminary Team

A preliminary team of experts and support personnel may be constituted by the *pourashavas* to assist in the process of prioritizing and selecting the public open space, identifying stakeholders, and outreach and building support for implementation. The *pourashavas* should also assess the existing and potential budget available for public open space development.

Activities	Who Leads the Process[a]	Supporting Personnel
Prioritize, select the public open space	Urban planner	At least one urban planner[b] and one landscape architect.
Identify and engage stakeholders	Social development or community development officer or gender equality or community engagement or community development specialist	Communications assistant

Notes:
[a] These may include staff in the *pourashavas*, or an external expert may be engaged.
[b] Geographic information system expertise is desirable.

1.2 Prioritize and Select a Public Open Space

The process for prioritizing and selecting a public open space (Figure 4) includes a comparative assessment based on four criteria: (i) community benefit; (ii) gender and social inclusion; (iii) environment, climate vulnerability, and adaptation; and (iv) landownership. The assessment can be supported by site photographs, maps, key informant interviews, group discussions, and other information.

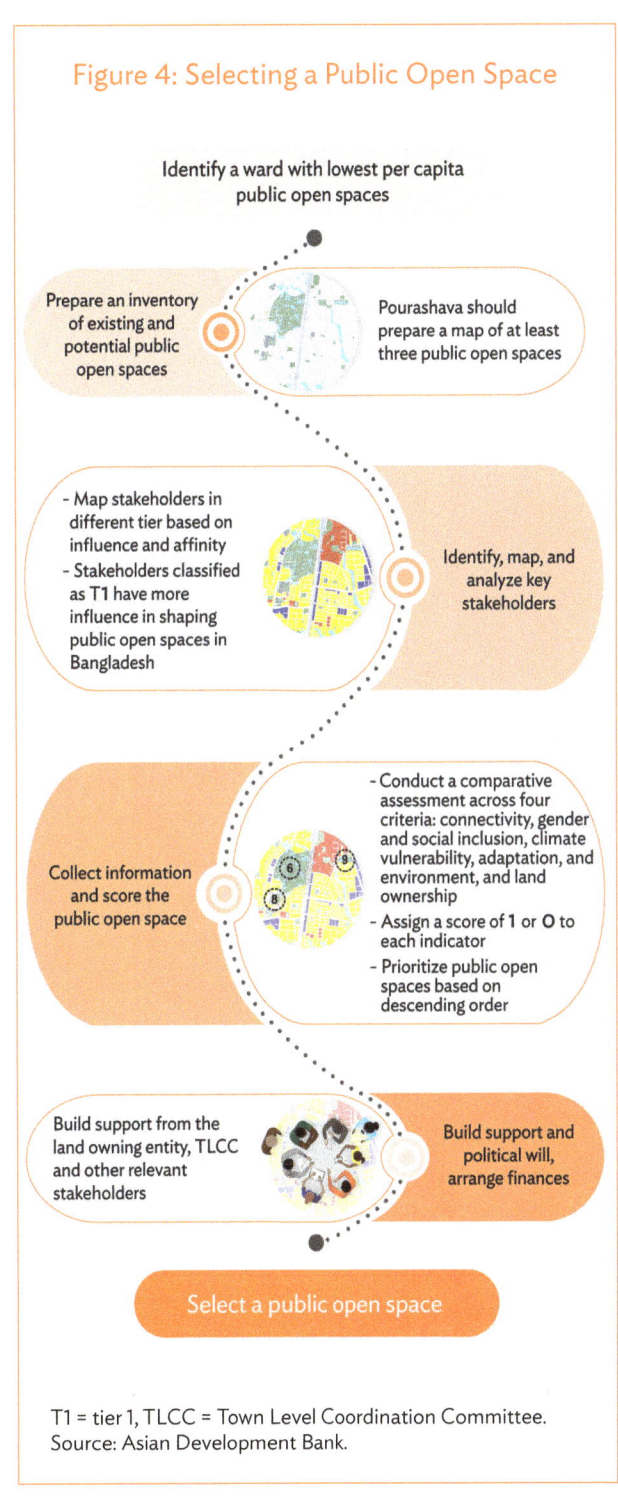

Figure 4: Selecting a Public Open Space

- Identify a ward with lowest per capita public open spaces
- Prepare an inventory of existing and potential public open spaces / Pourashava should prepare a map of at least three public open spaces
- Map stakeholders in different tier based on influence and affinity
- Stakeholders classified as T1 have more influence in shaping public open spaces in Bangladesh
- Identify, map, and analyze key stakeholders
- Collect information and score the public open space
  - Conduct a comparative assessment across four criteria: connectivity, gender and social inclusion, climate vulnerability, adaptation, and environment, and land ownership
  - Assign a score of 1 or 0 to each indicator
  - Prioritize public open spaces based on descending order
- Build support from the land owning entity, TLCC and other relevant stakeholders / Build support and political will, arrange finances
- Select a public open space

T1 = tier 1, TLCC = Town Level Coordination Committee.
Source: Asian Development Bank.

1.2.1 Prepare an inventory of existing and potential public open spaces.

The *pourashavas* should select a ward with the lowest public open space per capita in the city. If the ward does not have planned parks, gardens, or playgrounds, consider (a network of) underutilized or underdeveloped (public) land adjacent to public facilities and amenities, community pocket parks, streets (with a right-of-way less than 60 feet or 18 meters), nonmotorized transport pathways, road junctions, lakefronts, waterfronts, historical places, and monuments. It is recommended that the *pourashavas* prepare a map of at least three public open spaces.

1.2.2 Identify, map, and analyze key stakeholders.

A rapid, qualitative stakeholder mapping in different tiers is recommended based on influence and affinity (Figure 5). Institutions such as the Urban Development Directorate, the Local Government Engineering Department (LGED), and the *pourashavas* are classified as T1 stakeholders as they have more influence in shaping public open spaces in Bangladesh.

Civil society organizations, resident and business associations, schools, and religious committees are classified as T2 stakeholders as they may have lower influence, but more affinity to the public open space. The presence and influence of organizations like the Institute of Architects and the Bangladesh Institute of Planners in the *pourashavas* can be assessed.

The Local Government Department and Public Works Department may not have as much influence and affinity with public open space development and are categorized as T3 stakeholders.

1.2.3 Collect information and score the public open space.

The prioritization of the public open space projects is based on a comparative assessment across 4 criteria and 10 indicators (Table 1, Appendix 1-2). The data can be collected from secondary sources such as the master plan report; site observations; and interviews with community leaders, academics, and experts.

The indicators are assigned a score of 1 or 0. The public open spaces should be prioritized in a descending order of the scores.

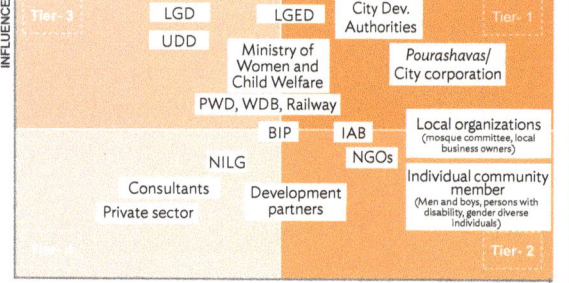

Figure 5: Stakeholder Mapping Based on Affinity and Influence

BIP = Bangladesh Institute of Planners, IAB = Institute of Architects and Builders, LGD = Local Government Department, LGED = Local Government Engineering Department, NGO = nongovernment organization, NILG = National Institute of Local Government, PWD = Public Works Department, UDD = Urban Development Directorate, WDB = Water Development Board.
Note: *Pourashava* is a term used for urban local bodies in towns in Bangladesh.
Source: UN-Habitat. 2020. *Public Space Site-Specific Assessment: Guidelines to Achieve Quality Public Spaces at Neighbourhood Level*. UN-Habitat.

Table 1: Criteria for Comparative Assessment of Public Open Spaces

Criteria	Summary of the Indicators
Connectivity	Public transport and paratransit connectivity and frequency.
Gender and social inclusion	Women and girls benefited; ethnic minority groups, informal settlements, and businesses are supported and not negatively impacted.
Climate vulnerability, adaptation, and environment	Vulnerability to climate risks, potential to provide refuge from cyclones, floods, and earthquakes and adopting nature-based solutions
Landownership	Land owned by the *pourashava* or a government agency

Source: Author.

1.2.4 Build support, political will, and arrange finances.

The *pourashavas* should garner support from the landowning entity, Town-Level Coordination Committee (TLCC), appropriate Standing Committees, other relevant government agencies, and current and potential users of the land. This can garner finances for the project, ease administrative approvals, enable integration with other social and

> **Box 1: Consider Constituting a Public Open Space Working Group**
>
> *Pourashavas* have coordination mechanisms such as the Town-Level Coordination Committee (TLCC), Ward-Level Standing Committee (WLCC), and Standing Committees. A public open space working group can be created to involve actors who are not part of the WLCC to meet regularly depending on the project need, advise the *pourashavas*, and facilitate buy-in between different government and nongovernment actors. The working group can include the following members, while aiming toward equal participation of women (including women with disabilities):
>
> (i) representative from *pourashavas* strategic management;
> (ii) representative from the Local Government Engineering Department;
> (iii) representative from the district administration;
> (iv) representative from the upazila administration;
> (v) representatives from the TLCC, WLCC, Standing Committees.;
> (vi) landowning entity;
> (vii) civil society organizations working with women, girls, persons with disabilities, public open spaces;
> (viii) academics and experts; and
> (ix) community leaders.
>
> There are numerous reasons why women and marginalized groups may not effectively participate in urban planning and governance. They could be intimidated, uninformed about the process or issues being discussed, and feel it is not relevant for them.[a] Targeted capacity development on urban planning, and governance and public open space development is required, an agenda for which is shared in Appendix 1-3.
>
> Note: *Pourashava* is a term used for urban local bodies in towns in Bangladesh.
>
> [a] G. Brown, P. Khan, and S. Hung, 2021. Gender-Responsive and Inclusive Urban Planning. In B. Susantono and R. Guild, eds. *Creating Livable Asian Cities*. pp. 89–106. Manila: Asian Development Bank.
>
> Source: Authors.

ecological elements within the larger network, and timely implementation of the project. Support from residents and businesses is crucial as they will be most impacted by it.

1.3 Assess and Strengthen the Capacity of the *Pourashava*

The development of public spaces requires technical and project management expertise at different stages of public open space design, implementation, and maintenance. The *pourashavas* should assess and strengthen its capacity, especially within the engineering departments, to effectively lead each stage while ensuring a participatory process that informs, involves, and collaborates with stakeholders. Different teams may be constituted to assign responsibility and ensure accountability. Team strength will depend upon the scale of the public open space and the type of *pourashavas* (A, B, or C).

Project management
Project management will be led by the engineering department of the *pourashavas*, and it can coordinate with the LGED and the landowning entity. Its role is to manage project timelines, implementation, and supervision.

Technical
The selection of the public open space, assessments, and preparation of a concept and detailed plan will be led by the engineering department of the *pourashavas*.

Multidisciplinary, short-term, experts in urban design, landscape, gender, universal access, sustainable infrastructure, and biodiversity are recommended to support the *pourashavas*. Junior architects and draftspersons may be required to provide additional support. The entire team must be trained on gender and social inclusion aspects to design effectively. The experts are listed as follows:

- Gender equality in landscape, urban design, planning
- Universal accessibility
- Sustainable infrastructure
- Biodiversity (desirable)
- Transport planner (required for street design projects)

Maintenance monitoring

The maintenance of a public open space usually lies with the *pourashavas*. Sometimes, other government organizations, such as the Zila Parishad or landowning agencies, may maintain the public open space. It is a long-term responsibility and requires fiscal and human resources. The engineering and/or conservancy department of the *pourashavas* can lead this process in coordination with the landowning entity and other organizations.

Communications

The conservancy, health, or engineering department within the *pourashavas* can lead communications and outreach, with the support of the social development officer or gender equality specialist and communications support personnel.

1.4 Prepare a Communications and Outreach Strategy

The preliminary stakeholder map created during site selection can be strengthened further with a stakeholder analysis table to understand their potential role and contribution (Appendix 1-4) in public open space improvement and create an engagement strategy.

A well-developed communications strategy can lead to effective engagement with targeted stakeholders based on their tier, role, and contribution in different stages (Appendix 1-5, Table 3). The strategy will depend on the kind of public participation envisioned. The *pourashavas* should aim to increase awareness, seek inputs, consistently involve and work jointly with stakeholders (Figure 6), and to develop communication methodss and tools to achieve the same (Figure 7).

A well-planned communication strategy addresses potential conflicts, helps raise public understanding, builds consensus, and generates informed dialogues. Communication tools can be used ranging from passive, one-way, to active, two-way, and multisensory engagement (Table 2). The outputs at different project stages and time frames, along with communication methods, are described.

Figure 6: Degrees of Public Participation

Source: Asian Development Bank.

Table 2: Illustrative Communication Tools

Tools
Newspapers
Audio announcements
Posters, banners, flyers
Presentations
3D simulations, before and after illustrations
Videos
Street plays
Radio, social media

(Passive to active)

Source: Authors.

Figure 7: Indicative Communication Methods at Each Project Stage

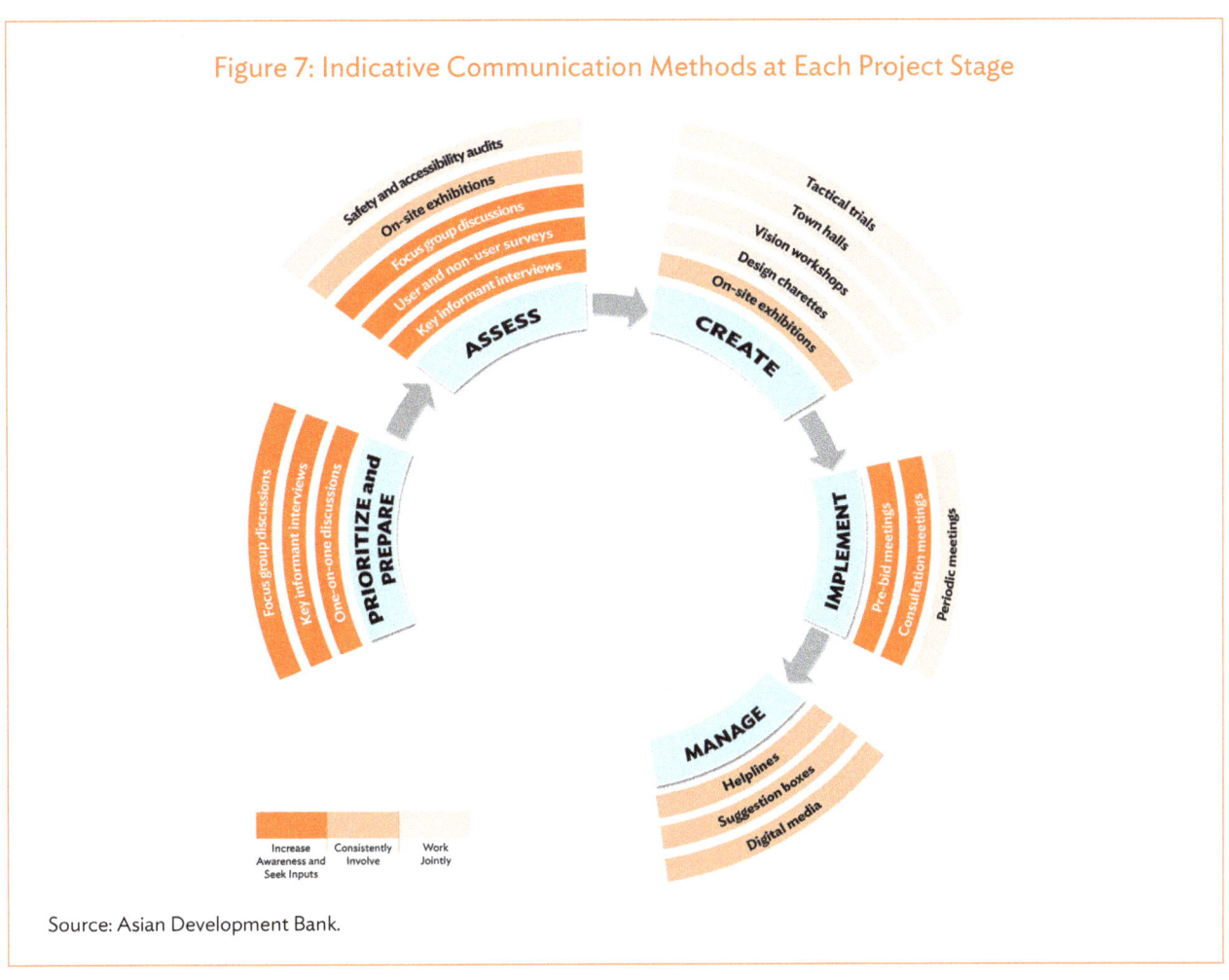

Source: Asian Development Bank.

Table 3: Stages, Outputs, and Indicative Communication Methods at Each Project Stage

Stages	Led by	Outputs (time in weeks)	Audiences	Suggested Communication Methods
Select the site	Technical team	• Project background, objectives, and impacts (6)	Resident and local community organizations; civil society organizations representing women, girls, gender minorities, and persons with disabilities; volunteers; and the working group	One-on-one discussions, key informant interviews, focus group discussions
Assess the public open space	Technical team	• Reconnaissance survey (4) • Existing Situation Analysis report (10)		Key informant interviews, user and non-user surveys, focus group discussions, safety and accessibility audits, on-site exhibitions
Create the design, validate, and test	Technical team	• Detailed concept plan report and tactical trial (12)		Design charrettes, visioning workshops, on-site exhibitions, town halls, tactical trial
Implement the design	Project management team	• Detailed project proposal and contract documents (8)	*Pourashavas*, advisory group, the concerned ministry	Pre-bid meetings, consultation meetings
Manage the public open space	Maintenance monitoring team	• Maintenance checklist (Prepared during the implementation stage)	*Pourashavas*, contractors, private sector	Helplines, suggestion boxes, and digital media

Source: Authors.

1.5 Prepare a Base Map and Conduct a Reconnaissance Survey

Prepare a base map of the public open space and its influence zone (400-meter walking distance) to understand the site and its surrounding characteristics. The process of base map preparation is outlined as follows:

- Geo-reference the site location using a satellite image or using a total station survey (Appendix 1-6).
- Map the road network, right-of-way, connectivity by different modes, and public transport stops.
- Map the formal and informal entrances/exits, disability access of the public open space along with its boundary and fencing.
- Map the landownership, adjacent land use, and major attractions such as public facilities and commercial centers.
- Conduct and use the total station survey to identify the amenities such as street furniture, streetlights, and public toilets.
- Map the natural features of the site such as the topography, vegetation, and water body.

A reconnaissance survey should be conducted to document the site and precinct through photographs. A detailed assessment should be conducted, the process of which is discussed in the next section.

A hypothetical public open space is taken to explain the assessments with reference pictures from the two-design brief prepared for Bagerhat and Kuakata.

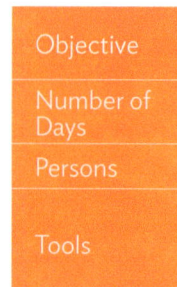

Objective	Conduct a reconnaissance survey of the public open space.
Number of Days	4 (including a weekday and weekends)
Persons	Led by the technical team
Tools	Notepad, base map, camera, or a phone with high-resolution photographs, pens

Figure 8: Example of a Base Map of a Public Open Space

m = meter.
Source: Asian Development Bank.

Public open space in Khulna Bangladesh. A boardwalk along the lake with shaded seating spaces (photo by Sonal Shah, ADB).

Assess

2.1 Assess the Local Blue Green–Gray Network and the Impact of Climate Risks on the Public Open Space

The 22 coastal towns in Bangladesh face climate risks including cyclones and coastal floods, river floods, water scarcity, extreme heat, and wildfire (ADB 2022).[2] It is important to understand climate risks at the metropolitan scale and how these impact the site and its surrounding precinct (photo, Table 4).

Precinct- and site-scale analyses also include assessing the continuity and capacity of local blue–green networks, micro-level catchment areas, site slopes (Figure 9), existing flora, and soil quality. This can assist in creating a road map and formulating strategies for adaptation.

Remote sensing, satellite imagery, and geographic information system (GIS) analysis can assist this process. Master plan and national disaster management reports, district disaster atlas, and the Disaster and Climate Risk Information Platform (DRIP)[3] can also be referred to (Appendix 2-1).

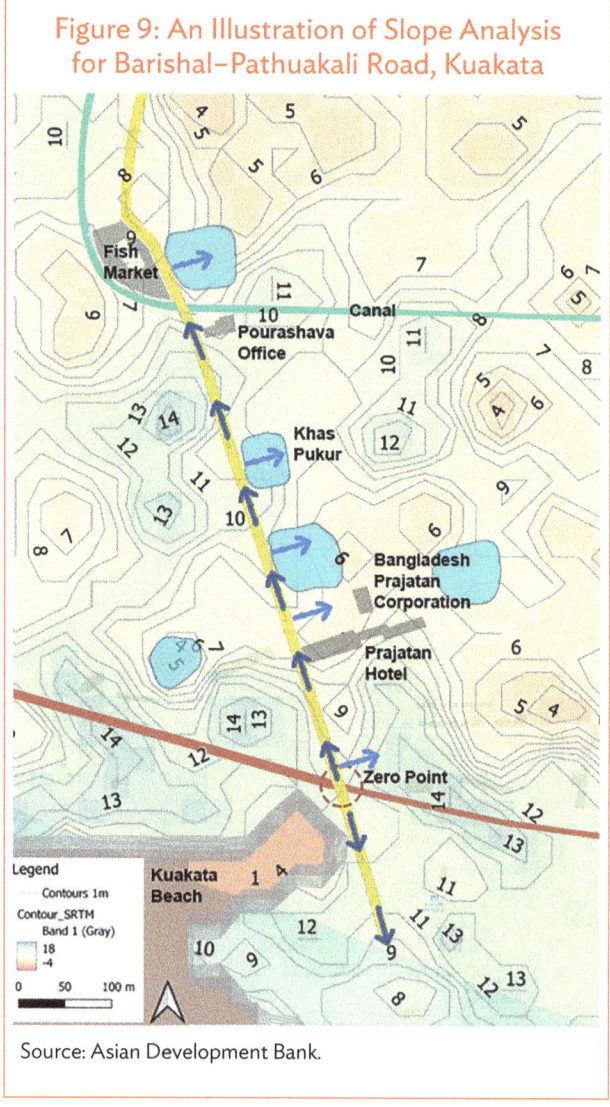

Figure 9: An Illustration of Slope Analysis for Barishal–Pathuakali Road, Kuakata

Source: Asian Development Bank.

Strategies to Adapt to Tidal Surges at Kuakata (photo by Sonal Shah, ADB).

---

[2] Part of the Coastal Towns Climate Resilience Project (CTCRP), funded by ADB.

[3] Government of Bangladesh, Disaster and Climate Risk Information Platform. Accessed 1 March 2023.

Table 4: Assessments for Various Hazards at the Metropolitan Region, Precinct, and Site Scales

Assessment	Questions	Cyclones, Coastal Floods	River Flood	Water Scarcity	Extreme Heat	Wildfire
Average Minimum and Maximum Temperature	What are the maximum/minimum temperatures and their seasonal variation?			✓	✓	✓
Annual and Peak Rainfall, Waterlogged Areas	What is the annual and peak rainfall? What is the duration of peak rainfall and which areas are waterlogged?	✓	✓	✓		
Land Cover	How much land area is developed, undeveloped, under forests, vegetation, and riverine area?	✓	✓		✓	✓
Sea Level Rise, Tidal Bore, Flood-Prone Areas	What are the areas vulnerable to sea level rise, tidal-prone, and flood-prone areas?	✓	✓			
Watershed	How does the regional watershed impact the precinct?	✓	✓	✓		
Cyclone-Prone Area and Cyclone Shelter Locations	Where are the high-risk cyclone-prone areas? Where and what is the existing number of cyclone shelters?	✓	✓			✓
Embankment Erosion-Prone Areas	What is the rate of riverbank erosion, and level of salinity intrusion?	✓	✓			
Blue-Green Cover Network and Micro-watershed	How continuous and connected is the blue-green network, and what is the micro-watershed?	✓	✓	✓		✓
Stormwater Network	How is the stormwater drainage and water runoff network?	✓	✓			
Slope Analysis	What is the land topography, high and low-lying areas, and how are they impacted by disasters?	✓	✓	✓		
Soil Quality (Salinity intrusion etc)	What are the types of soil, and contaminants in the soil?	✓	✓	✓	✓	✓
Vegetation Inventory	What are the types of local vegetation to enhance climate adaptation?	✓	✓	✓	✓	✓
Aquifer Zones	What is the groundwater level and what are the opportunities for aquifer recharging?	✓	✓	✓	✓	

■ Additional assessment at the precinct and site scales.

Note: Other hazards can be included based on the location of the city.

Source: Authors.

2.2 Conduct a Detailed Assessment of the Public Open Space

Objective	Conduct a detailed assessment of the public open space.
Number of Days	5 (including a weekday and weekend)
Persons	Led by the technical team
Tools	Notepad, base map, camera or a phone with high-resolution photographs, voice recorder, pens

A detailed assessment aims to collect information through stakeholder engagement and document the public open space through digital media, i.e., photography and videography; and non-digital media, i.e., hand-drawn sketches and notes. This data can be used to update the base map prepared from secondary desk research. A comprehensive **quality assessment** of connectivity, walkability, safety, amenities and furniture, environment and heritage, and lighting should be conducted (Appendix 2-8). The key tasks are as follows:

Stakeholder engagement
Engage T1 and T2 stakeholders, existing and potential users of the public open space.

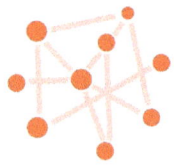

Connectivity and access
Understand and map the street network for pedestrians, public transport, paratransit connectivity, and access.

Spatial context and mapping
Map the landmarks, attractors, activities, and uses of the public open space within 400-meter walking distance.

Existing climate adaptation interventions
Observe the existing drainage system, and existing and proposed climate mitigation and adaptation interventions.

Safety and security
Assess the measures adopted by the public open space for safety and security.

Street furniture and amenities
Identify and map the condition and demand of the existing public amenities and street furniture.

Universal and gender-responsive design
Identify and map the design initiatives for gender-responsive and universal access.

Placemaking
Identify and photo document the visual, and sensory experience of the public open space.

Information and communications
Observe and map the signage, public information, and communication messages.

Events
Identify and list the festivals, cultural practices, and beliefs, which may determine the design of the public open space.

2.2.1 Stakeholder engagement

The objective is to introduce the project to T1 and T2 stakeholders (Appendix 2-2). This will include user surveys (Appendix 2-3), focus group discussions (Appendix 2-4) with civil society organizations and T2 stakeholders representing women, girls, gender minorities, and persons with disabilities; key informant interviews with T1 and T2 stakeholders to assess their knowledge, attitude, and practices (Appendix 2-5); and surveys with occasional or non-users of the public open space (Appendix 2-6).

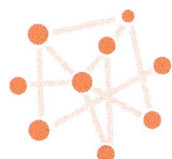

2.2.2 Connectivity and access

The key questions to be addressed during the assessment (Figure 10) are:

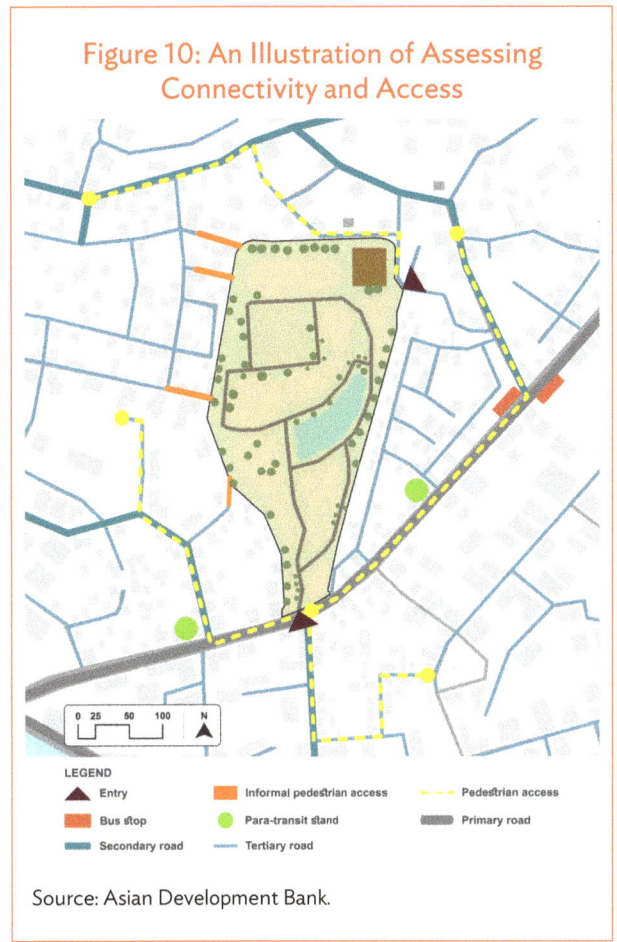

Figure 10: An Illustration of Assessing Connectivity and Access

Source: Asian Development Bank.

Connectivity	How is the public open space connected to the surrounding road network, pedestrian pathways?
Frequency	How frequent is the existing public transport, paratransit and how far is the nearest public transport stop?
Safety and security	How safe is the access for pedestrians and cyclists of all age groups and persons with disabilities? How safe and secure do women and girls feel in accessing the public open space?

The key assessments (Appendix 2-8) include:

- **Street and public transport network**
  Map the street hierarchy, public transport, paratransit routes, services and stops, and pedestrian and cycling pathways, infrastructure; draw street sections of the access streets.
- **Access points**
  Map the entrances/exits to the public open space, including formal and informal access points.
- **Universal and gender-responsive design**
  Map and photo document the quality of accessibility to the public open space for persons with limited mobility, vision, hearing, and neurodivergent persons.

2.2.3 Spatial context and mapping

The assessment will involve mapping, sketching, and photo documentation of the public open space five times in a day: early morning, morning, afternoon, evening, and night (Figure 11). It should include a weekday, a weekend, and festivals where relevant. The key questions are:

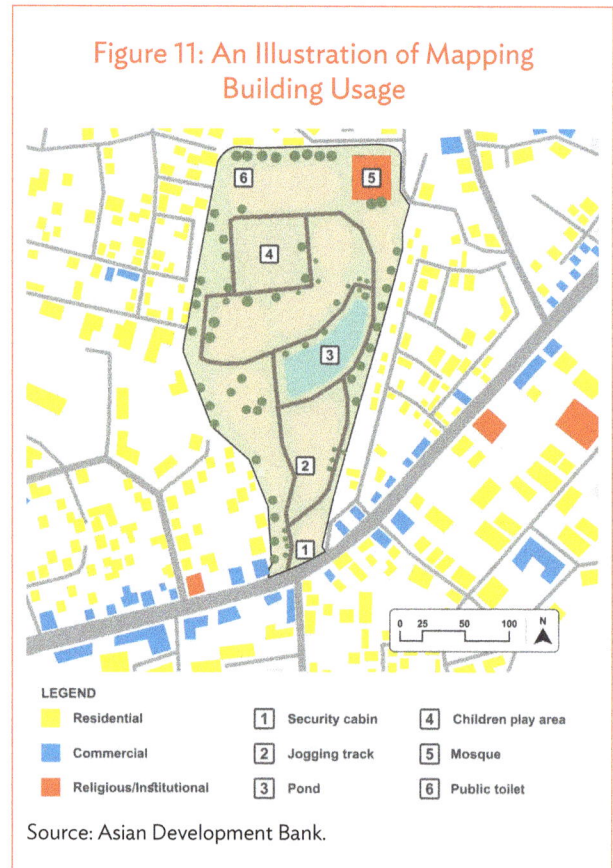

Figure 11: An Illustration of Mapping Building Usage

LEGEND
- Residential
- Commercial
- Religious/Institutional
- [1] Security cabin
- [2] Jogging track
- [3] Pond
- [4] Children play area
- [5] Mosque
- [6] Public toilet

Source: Asian Development Bank.

Land use, major attractors	What are the land use, landmarks, and major attractors in and around the public open space?
Activities	What are the different spatial and temporal activities in the public open space?

The spatial and temporal activities and use of the public open space can be assessed using activity maps, age, and gender counts. The key questions for **spatial activity maps** should include:

Activities and time	How do people use the public open space at different times?
Gender, age, ability differences	What is the difference in the use of the public open space between men, women, gender minorities, and persons with disabilities, and across age and income groups? Who is underrepresented?
Conflicts	What are the existing and potential conflicts (e.g., example, between pedestrians and vehicles)?

Spatial activity maps can be created for 1 day of the week, Friday and Saturday, and special events. The public open space should be documented at the following times, or as determined based on the reconnaissance survey:

- Early morning: Before 8 a.m.
- Morning: 8 a.m. to 12 noon
- Afternoon: 12 noon to 4 p.m.
- Evening: 4 p.m. to 8 p.m.
- Night: After 8 p.m.

Age and gender counts (including those with impairments) can be done at 15-minute intervals over 1 hour in each time zone (Appendix 2-7, Figure 12).

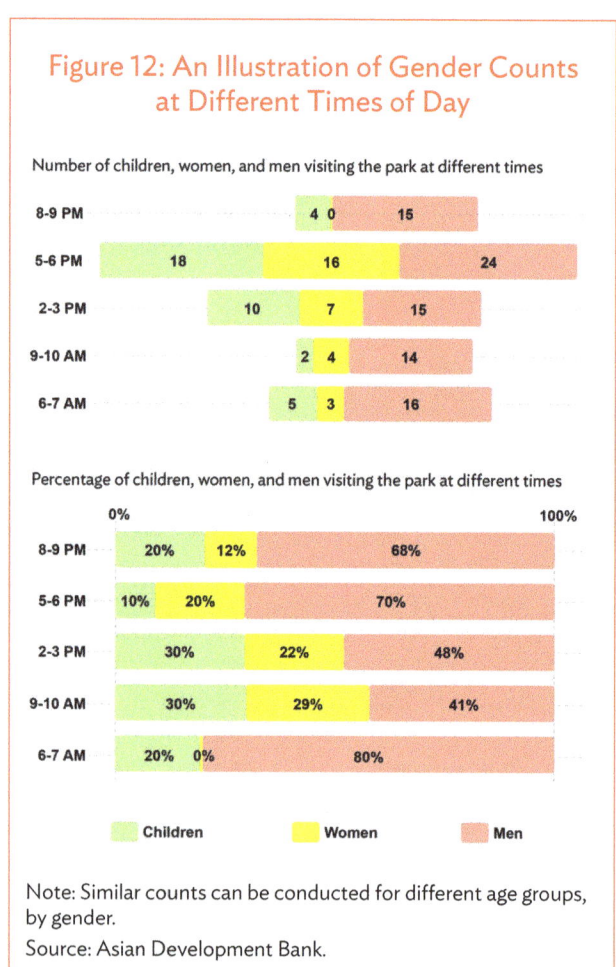

Figure 12: An Illustration of Gender Counts at Different Times of Day

Note: Similar counts can be conducted for different age groups, by gender.
Source: Asian Development Bank.

2.2.4 Existing climate adaptation interventions

The objective is to assess the effect of climate risks on the public open space and adaptation measures (Appendix 2-8, Figure 13). The key questions are:

Climate risks	How do existing climate risks impact the public open space?
Climate adaptation interventions	What are the climate adaptation interventions and what is their impact?
Vegetation	What is the type of existing green cover in the public open space and what are the species?

Figure 13: An Illustration of Assessing Climate Adaptation Interventions

Source: Asian Development Bank.

This assessment will include photo documentation, sketching a cross-section of the open space, a map of the existing water bodies, catchment areas, vegetation, embankments, and existing flood mitigation measures. Obtain feedback from the disaster management committee at this juncture.

2.2.5 Safety and security

Safety and security assessments include road safety, gendered safety, and safety from crime. The perception and experience for women, girls, and gender minorities is different from that of men and boys due to concerns of sexual exploitation, abuse, and harassment. The planning and design of public open spaces can influence the perception of safety. The public open space can be mapped, and photo documented at different times of the day and night to understand the following (Appendix 2-8, Figure 14):

Perception and experience of sexual abuse and harassment	User survey (Appendix 2-3) and non-user survey (Appendix 2-6) by age and incomes to understand the gendered experiences of abuse and harassment.
Active, crowds, secluded areas	How active, secluded, or crowded is the public open space in the day and night? Are areas dominated by men and boys?
Blind spots	Are there any blind spots that make the public open space unsafe?
Dark corners	Is the public open space well illuminated or are there dark, invisible corners in the evening and night?
Amenities	How safe is the access to public toilets and amenities?

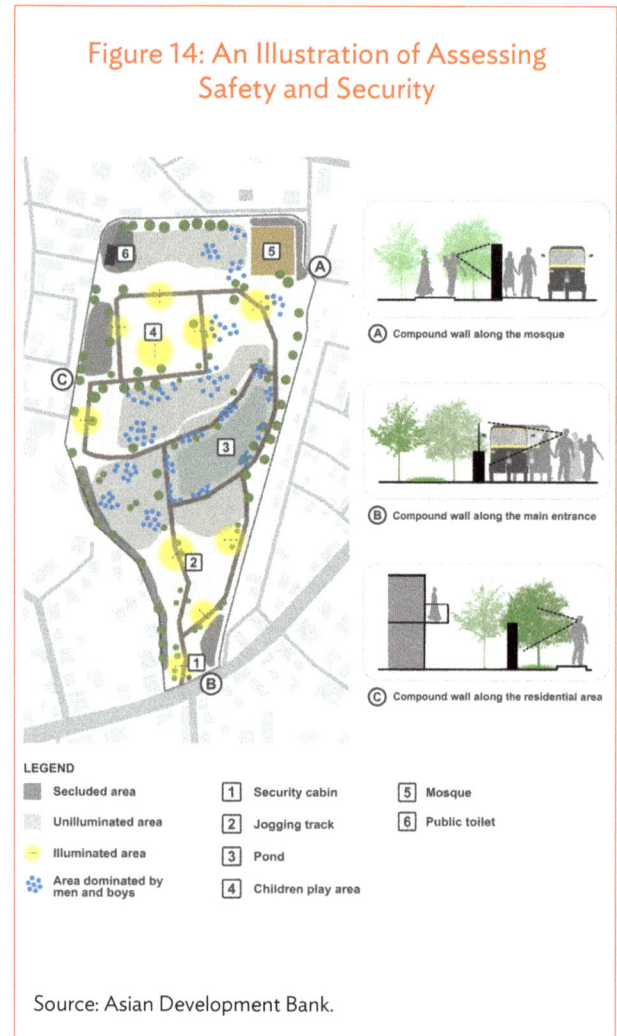

Figure 14: An Illustration of Assessing Safety and Security

Source: Asian Development Bank.

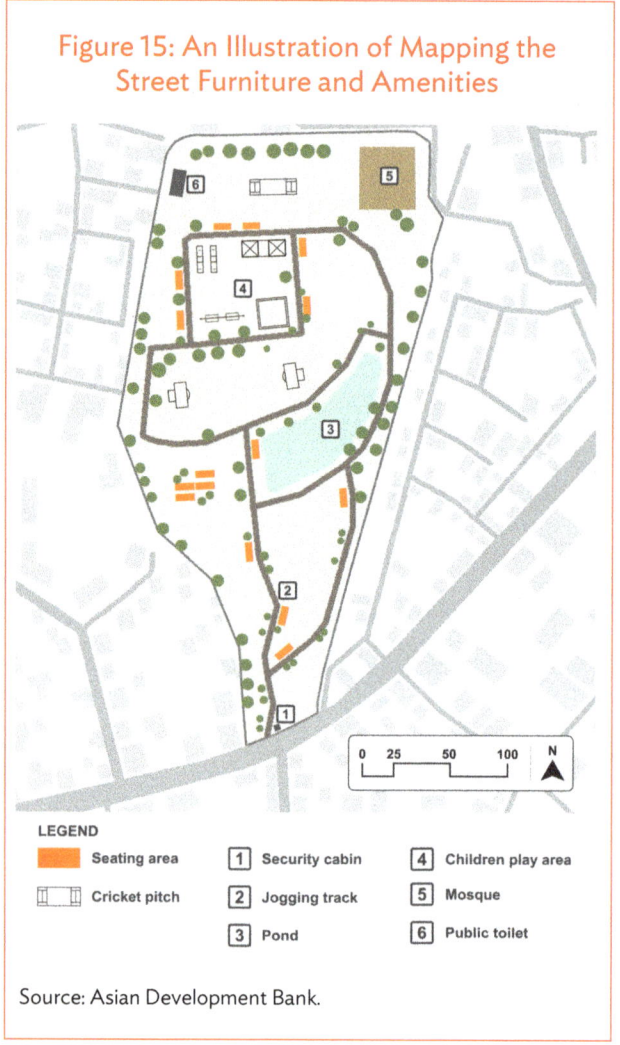

Figure 15: An Illustration of Mapping the Street Furniture and Amenities

Source: Asian Development Bank.

2.2.6 Street furniture and amenities

This includes mapping and photo documentation of street furniture and their location, adequacy, and intervals: garbage bins, seating, and streetlights; amenities such as information and grievance redress center, public toilets, nursing space, creche, livelihood or skill development center, nursery, play equipment for different age groups, play areas for infants, toddlers, and adolescent girls, quiet spaces for persons with autism, drinking water; and the presence of security guards and caretakers (Appendix 2-8, Figure 15).

2.2.7 Universal and gender-responsive design

This focuses on identifying barriers and existing design interventions for persons with limited mobility, visibility, and hearing; and neurodivergent persons. Outline a journey route, map, and photo document the path and elements provided in the public open space (Appendix 2-8). The key questions are:

Pre-planning	Does the public open space provide adequate, accessible pre-planning information?
Accessibility	How accessible are pathways, public toilets, street furniture;and amenities for pregnant women, caregivers, persons with limited motion, hearing, vision, and neurodivergent persons?[4]
Sensitization	How are the public open space personnel sensitized on behaving with persons with disabilities, being observant to and addressing abuse and harassment faced by women with disabilities?
Quiet areas	Does the public open space have a designated space for neurodivergent persons?

2.2.8 Placemaking

Placemaking entails creating a unique experience for users. This can be assessed to understand the perceptions and experience of the public open space through different senses (Appendix 2-3). The history and contribution of women leaders and women workers can be documented and expressed. Photo document and sketch visual corridors or vistas, architectural elements and materials, and sensory experience of the public open space. The key questions for the placemaking assessment are:

Architecture language	What is the architectural language (design elements and materials) of the city, precinct, and community?
Sensory experience	How can the public open space be experienced through different senses and to highlight the contribution of women workers and leaders?

Visual language	Do the art, advertisements, and visual language communicate positive gender norms and socialization?

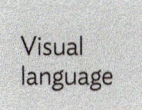

2.2.9 Information and communications

This involves mapping and documenting the different types of information and signage. The key questions are:

Channels of information	What are the different channels of information about the public open space; reporting sexual exploitation, abuse, and harassment (SEAH); and are they accessible for persons with all abilities?
Address SEAH	How can SEAH be reported and what is the process for addressing it?
Signage system	What is the signage system for directions and wayfinding, safety, emergency, and general information? Is it gender balanced?

2.2.10 Events

Interview the *pourashavas* to understand the events organized by them, especially to increase the use of the public open space for women, adolescent girls, and persons with disabilities. Additionally, observe and engage with users to understand regular, periodic, or cultural events. These include weddings, community gatherings, festivals such as the Buddha Purnima festival, and other cultural activities.

---

[4] Such as drinking water fountains and seating areas.

2.3 Conduct Participatory Safety Audits

Women's safety audit is a tool that increases awareness of gender-based violence in public spaces. It helps users and decision-makers understand the gendered experience of the urban environment, legitimize women's safety concerns, and is an effective tool for building community safety (UN-Habitat 2009).

Participatory safety audit with women and girls in Bagerhat (photo by Sarah Hui Li, ADB).

Objective	Understand and map issues of safety and comfort in terms of infrastructure and design, and map harassment faced in public spaces.
Number of hours	3.0–3.5 hours: To be conducted in the evening or at night. Safe travel arrangements should be made for participants.
Persons	Led by the technical team: 5 persons (lead the walk, photo document the walk, and 3 persons to provide support to the participants), 8–10 local participants. Consider organizing separate walks for different economic groups of women, poor women workers, adolescent girls, and gender minorities.
Tools	Safety audit checklist (Appendix 2-9), street map, camera, pens.

A safety audit includes an orientation workshop with different target groups and volunteers to familiarize them with the objectives and methodology of the safety audit walk and the questionnaire (photo). This should be followed by a debriefing session to determine safety walk scores for different aspects of the public open space, a gender safety and violence map, and prioritize issues and brainstorm possible solutions.

2.4 Conduct Participatory Accessibility Audits

Objective	Understand and map issues of accessibility and comfort for persons with disabilities in terms of infrastructure, design, and support.
Number of hours	2 (both daytime and nighttime audits must be conducted).
Persons	Led by the technical team: three persons (lead the walk, shoot a video, and manage the group); three persons with limited physical, visual, and hearing; and three facilitators (especially a sign language interpreter). Organize a separate walk with women and girls with disabilities.
Tools	Accessibility audit checklist (Appendix 2-10), street map, cameras, pens.

The accessibility audit is conducted to identify barriers that persons with disabilities encounter in public spaces. The audit includes an orientation workshop with the participants to familiarize them with the objectives and methodology of the accessibility audit and the questionnaire. After the accessibility audit, organize a debriefing session to identify priority issues and brainstorm possible solutions (photo). The accessibility audit can be supplemented by focus group discussions and in-depth interviews with the participants. It is useful to capture a video recording of the accessibility audit with a person in a wheelchair, and with limited visibility and hearing, in addition to photographs and observation notes.

2.5 Understand the Barriers and Expectations of Diverse Groups

On-site exhibitions can be used to understand the barriers and prioritize expectations of users on-site (Appendix 2-11).

- **Barriers:** The physical and social barriers that inhibit different groups of women and girls and persons with disabilities from accessing and using a public open space.
- **Expectations:** Understanding and prioritizing expectations may be related to safety and security, resilience to climate risks, well-maintained amenities, and street furniture.

Participatory Accessibility Audit with the Users of the Park in Bagerhat (photo by Sarah Hui Li, ADB).

> **Box 2: Ethical Considerations**
>
> Throughout the stakeholder engagement process, due diligence will be maintained particularly regarding the local culture and customs. Personal identities will be withheld. The aim of the activities will be clearly explained before every exercise. Stakeholders and the interviewers and/or stewards will be on equal terms in terms of power dynamics. The researchers and/or interviewers are not superior or in a position of power relative to the stakeholders, thus truly exercising the essence of the inclusive design process.
>
> A variety of topics on gender-based violence and sexual exploitation, abuse, and harassment will be discussed with the stakeholders. These will include, but not be limited to, verbal abuse such as eve teasing, and physical abuse including groping, rape, and murder. It is of utmost importance to initiate and maintain these discussions with proper consent, confidentiality, and sensitivity without putting the women, or gender-minority person in any form of risk or harm. Participants' safety, confidentiality, and comfort should be of the highest importance during violence-related exercises. It is important to be a good listener, patient and nonjudgmental during interactions and experience sharing. A detailed guide on how to conduct gender-based violence sessions by Namati can be found here: https://namati.org/resources/training-manual-on-gender-based-violence/.
>
> Materials and discussions should include and highlight the existing violence reporting mechanisms of the Government of Bangladesh, such as the National Helpline Centre for Violence Against Women and Children hotline 109, police hotline 999; district-level One Stop Crisis Centres where available, Women's Affairs Officers, and Legal Support Offices. For more details on violence reporting and support, please see National Helpline Centre for Violence against Women and Children.[a]
>
> All the enumerators and facilitators should be trained in ethical considerations, and separate focus group discussions should be organized with women, girls, persons with disabilities, and gender minorities.
>
> [a] Government of Bangladesh, Department of Women Affairs. National Helpline Centre for Violence against Women and Children: http://nhc.gov.bd/.
>
> Source: Authors.

Visioning Workshop. This workshop engaged the community to develop a vision for the public open space in their neighborhood in Bagerhat (photo by Sarah Hui Li, ADB).

Create

3.1 Facilitate a Multistakeholder Visioning Workshop

Organize participatory design charrette with users, government, and nongovernment stakeholders on the future vision and design of the street, walkway, park, garden, and playground (photo). This can be planned as a day-long session, with about 50–70 people. The first half of the session can focus on presenting the objective of the project and the assessments. The second half of the session can focus on the envisioning and design exercise (Appendix 3-1).

Participants can include civil society organizations representing women, girls, gender minorities, persons with disabilities, schools, colleges, cultural and religious institutions, and youth clubs. A gender balance should be ensured among the participants.

3.2 Create a Concept Plan

The concept plan includes strategies to reduce ecological vulnerability; address gaps in safety and accessibility and amenities; and improve comfort for women, girls, gender minorities, people with disabilities, older people, and livelihood workers.

3.2.1 Improve climate adaptation.

A. Create a local water management network plan.

Mitigate the impact of floods, and water overflow with the following strategies: spread the flow of water to adjoining public open spaces; soak, retain, or detain the water; and reconnect the overflow to the stormwater network. This can be used as a basis for partnership with other agencies for the availability of funds or implementation (Figure 16).

Stakeholder Visioning Workshop in Bagerhat and Kuakata (photo by Md. Habib Ullah, ADB).

Explore technologies to conserve and store (sweet) water, rainwater harvesting, and reduce water consumption by recycling wastewater and through ecological sanitation (eco-toilets or dry toilets).

B. Adopt contextually relevant climate adaptation design strategies.

Streets, parks, and playgrounds located along beaches, mangroves, rivers, canals, and lakes can be protected through the following design strategies (Table 5).

C. Design strategies to reduce soil salinity.

Salinity intrusion has adverse effects on water, soils, ecosystem, and livelihoods in Bangladesh. The salinity of the soil can be reduced through adaptive measures such as installing injection wells, mulching for growing vegetables, and selecting salt-tolerant varieties of crops for urban community horticulture. These include rice varieties such as Jotabalam, Aashfall, Ghunshi, and Benapol, and some rain trees such as Babla, Khoiba-bla, Tentul, Kewra, Coconut, Koroi, Khejur, and Paroshpipul (Habiba, Abedin, Shaw, and Hassan 2014).

D. Design strategies to remove water impurities and soak the water.

Bioswales, permeable pavements, and tree trenches can be considered along with redesigning stormwater drains and filtration gravel beds to remove impurities and allow clean water to pass through the drain.

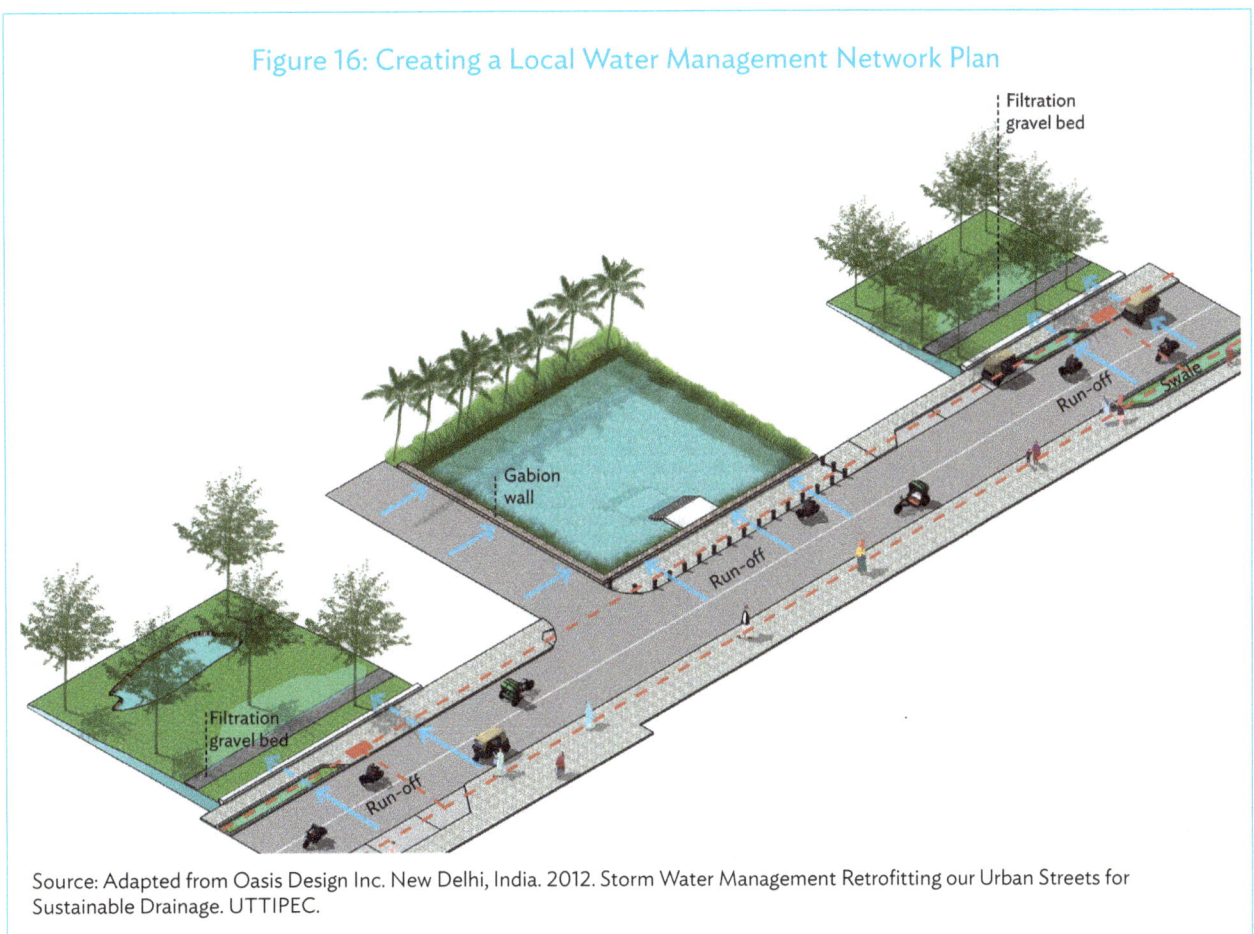

Figure 16: Creating a Local Water Management Network Plan

Source: Adapted from Oasis Design Inc. New Delhi, India. 2012. Storm Water Management Retrofitting our Urban Streets for Sustainable Drainage. UTTIPEC.

Access to public open space. An enbankment along the lake edge at Cultural Club, Bagerhat (photo by Muhammad Shamsuzzaman, ADB).

Table 5: Objectives and Strategies to Strengthen Climate Adaptation

Natural Edge	Beach	Mangroves	Rivers, Canals, and Lakes
Objectives	Prevent beach erosion, reduce tidal surges and wave velocity.	Restore mangroves, improve water salinity, and cyclone safety.	Prevent soil erosion and flooding and provide room for the river along undeveloped edges.
Strategies	• Embankments, and nature-based solutions like groins, and breakwaters and sea walls • Assisted natural reforestation on the beach	• Assisted natural reforestation with boardwalks • Combination of soft and gray solutions by using bamboo structures and small stone dikes to trap sediment and attenuate swell before reforestation • Some species relevant for coastal areas include Keora, Korai, Genoa trees, Amaranth, and fruit species like Sofeda and Peyara	Upstream • Vetiver plants for slope stabilization • Assisted natural reforestation on the edges to avoid erosion Downstream • Canals to connect with rivers and sea to create a passage and store water • Accessible embankments along river edges • Mudflats along the rivers and sea • Stormwater drain cleaning and improvement Longer-term strategies • Buffer zones along rivers and canals in development control measures

continued on next page

Table 5 continued

Illustrative Examples

Groins
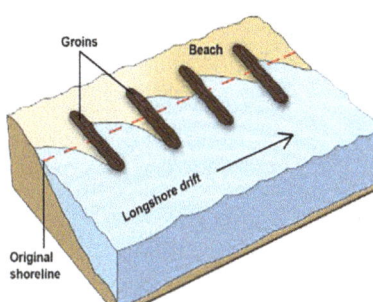

Forestation between breakwaters
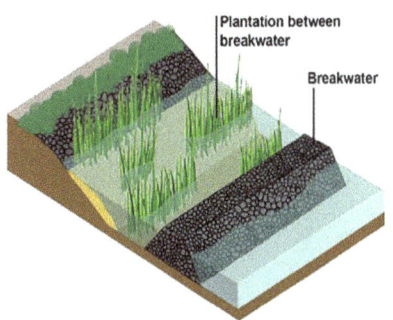

Slope stabilization using vetiver plant
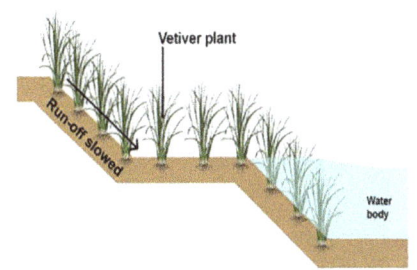

Breakwaters
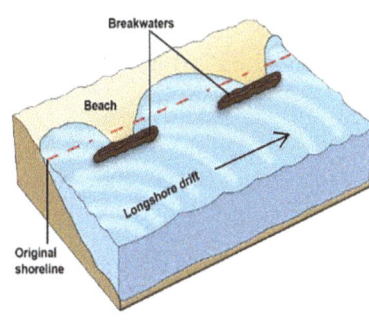

Sediment trap and wave attenuation structure
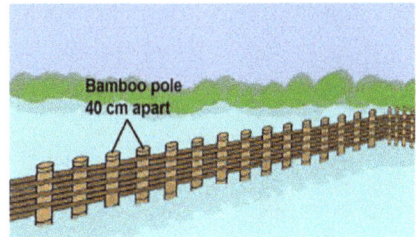

Mudflat along rivers and coastal areas for slope stabilization
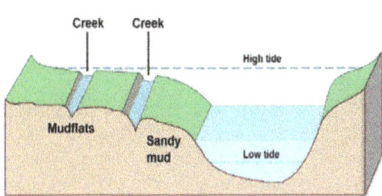

Seawall at Kuakata Beach

Source: Sonal Shah, ADB.

Boardwalk along mangroves
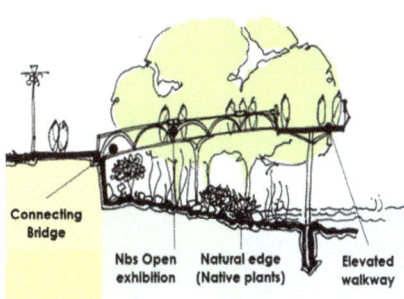

Source: Apoorv Garg, ADB.

Stepped embankment along a lake edge at Khan Jahan Ali Mazar, Bagerhat

Source: Md. Habib Ullah, ADB.

ADB = Asian Development Bank.
Source: Authors.

E. Recommended vegetation.

The following list of trees and shrubs can be considered in coastal saline areas in Bangladesh (Figure 17). The planting strategy should consider visibility and not create unsafe spaces for women and girls.

Figure 17: Trees and Shrubs for Coastal Towns

Source: Asian Development Bank.

3.2.2 Improve connectivity and accessibility.

Overall

Pedestrian facilities	Design well-lit, unobstructed, shaded, and accessible footpaths around the public open space, with safe mid-block crossings and intersections (Figure 18).
Public transport	Improve public transport connectivity and frequency (where feasible), gender-responsive bus stops, and accessibility. Consider reserved seats for women and girls, low-floor buses, and level boarding.
Pickup and drop-off	Provide shaded pickup and drop-off points for paratransit vehicles, and cycle parking.
Universal access	Include access ramps, anti-skid surfaces, maintain levelled footpaths, ensure consistency of color and texture.

Streets: Redesign streets to prioritize and provide safe and accessible pedestrian and cycling facilities, mid-block and intersection crossings; consider nonmotorized transport-only streets for weekly markets and retail streets with high pedestrian footfall.

Footpaths	Provide footpaths on all roads above 12 meters (m).
Cycle tracks	Provide cycle tracks (2.5 m for one-way and 5 m for two-way) for all roads above 24 m; and traffic calm streets to less than 30 kilometers per hour for roads without cycle tracks.
Carriageway	Ensure a consistent carriageway considering the narrowest section of the right-of-way.
Mid-block crossings	Provide accessible mid-block crossings with pedestrian refuge at intervals of 100 m to 150 m.
Intersections	Consider raised intersections for non-signalized intersections; provide pedestrian refuge and safe spaces for cyclists to wait at intersections.
Traffic signals	Consider green phases for pedestrians and cyclists; ensure that the traffic signals consider crossing times for caregivers, older people, and people with disabilities.
On-street parking	Reorganize and consider paid on-street parking in areas with high demand.

Parks, playgrounds, gardens, tot lots

Nonmotorized transport access — Provide nonmotorized pathways through the public open space and connect it to the public street network, to reduce walking and cycling distances.

Universal and gender-responsive design[5]

Information — Provide information on the *pourashavas* website to understand which part of the park, garden, and playground is accessible.

Public transport — Create an accessible public transport system with level boarding, audiovisual information, and reserved seats for people with disabilities, accessible bus stops, and footpaths (Appendix 3-2).

Pedestrian facilities — Create accessible footpaths and walkways with anti-skid surfaces, uninterrupted walkways, guiding and warning pavers, and access ramps at a ratio of 1:12.

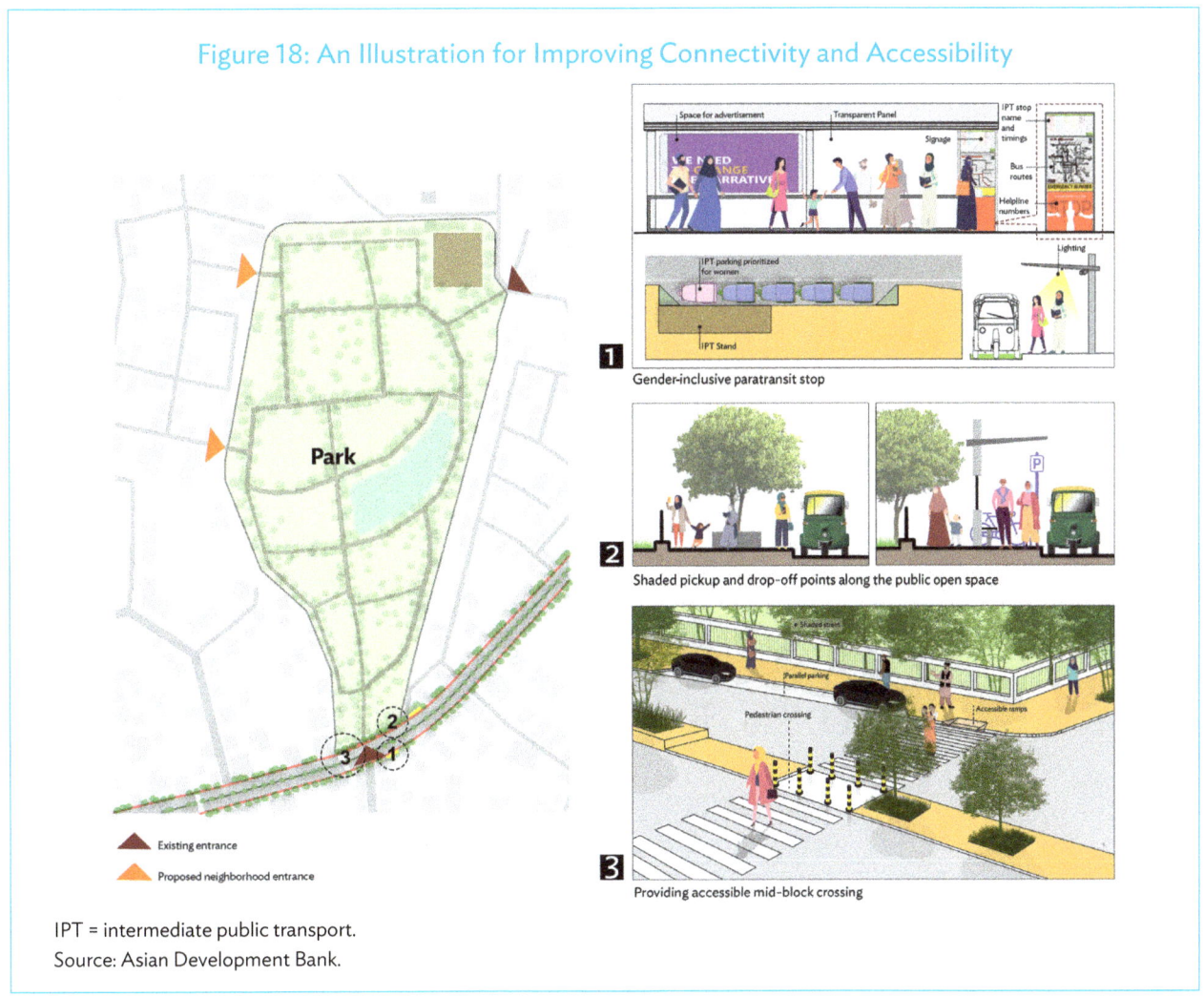

Figure 18: An Illustration for Improving Connectivity and Accessibility

1. Gender-inclusive paratransit stop
2. Shaded pickup and drop-off points along the public open space
3. Providing accessible mid-block crossing

IPT = intermediate public transport.
Source: Asian Development Bank.

---

[5] A twin-track approach should be considered. The objective is to mainstream accessibility in the design. However, in cases where there is stigma and women with disabilities are unsafe, or their participation may increase with peers, then targeted events or segregated spaces may be considered.

3.2.3 Create a layout plan for different activities.

Parks, gardens, playgrounds, tot lots

The activity map can encourage flexible use of the public open space, and it can be used by both boys and girls, children, older people, and people with disabilities (Table 6, Figure 19, Figure 20, Appendix 3-2).

Structured and unstructured activities	Plan the space for structured and unstructured activities; consider trees and shrubs, mounds to break up large natural grass areas. This prevents the most assertive groups from occupying large areas. It can facilitate simultaneous use by several different groups (Tbilisi Municipality 2021); provide access ramps in lawns and play areas.
Active, passive use	Plan for active and passive use such as walking, strolling, play and resting, waiting, sitting, and meditation; provide access ramps in lawn areas.
Activity center	Consider an activity center to organize activities for children, women, girls, gender minorities, and people with disabilities.
Amenities	Locate street furniture and amenities such as drinking water fountains, seating, public toilets, and nursing rooms in well-lit and well-accessed areas; ensure gender-responsive and universal access; consider quiet zones for persons with autism (Appendix 3_2).
Emergency	Plan for emergencies considering disaster risk management plans.

Table 6: Design Criteria for Different Age Groups

Age (years)	Activity	Design Considerations
0–10	Play, caretaker supervision	• Locate children's play areas at a distance from those that involve games such as cricket and football. • Play equipment for children of different age groups and abilities. • Provide natural ground-like sand pit areas, mounds, or grass surfaces. • Play objects should have soft surfaces. • Shaded and green/planting area with resting spaces should be provided. • A low fence to protect infants and toddlers. • Provide seating and exercise equipment for caregivers in proximity for supervision of the toddlers.
10–19	Playground, play areas, sitting space	• Consider designated active play areas for girls and activities that may be popular with them. These include, but are not limited to, badminton, throwball, handball, and volleyball. • Consider exercise equipment. • Play equipment for children of different abilities. • Provide ball catch fences and nets if a court is next to a street.
Older people, persons with different abilities	Quiet, accessible, and shaded sitting space	• Ensure pathways have access ramps and guiding pavers. • Visual cues and tactile cues should provide information about location and pathways so that older people can orient themselves and navigate with ease. • Sensual exploration to cater to people with a sensory impairment (visual, auditory, kinesthetic). • Provide raised flower beds and gardens for viewing and gardening without stooping. • Game zones increases elderly people's physical and mental activities, which helps improve their memory, attention, and concentration. • Natural surveillance and visibility of open space.

Source: Authors.

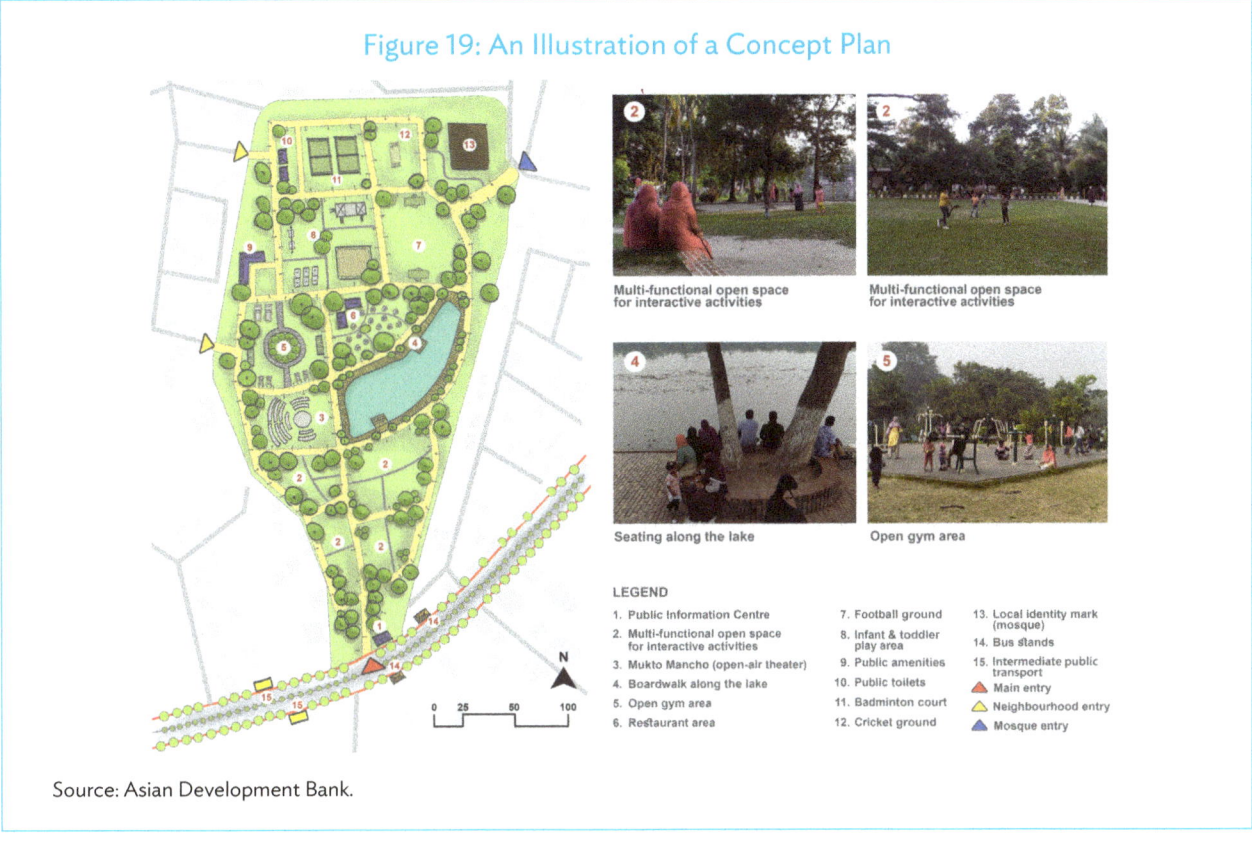

Figure 19: An Illustration of a Concept Plan

Source: Asian Development Bank.

Figure 20: Before and After Rendering of a Pathway in Rupa Chaudhary Pouro Park

Source: Asian Development Bank.

3.2.4 Improve safety and security.

Streets

Speed management	Improve road safety through speed limits not exceeding 30 kilometers per hour (kph) and regulate speeds through traffic calming measures such as raised unsignalized intersections and tabletop crossings.

Streets, parks, playgrounds, gardens, tot lots:
Address gender safety through the following strategies (Figure 21):

Information	Provide accessible information boards (Appendix 3-1) with maps of the park, clearly displaying existing helpline numbers.
Visibility	Ensure visibility and lines of sight along the edges, when selecting vegetation and throughout the public open space.
Illumination	Ensure activity-appropriate, energy-efficient, and uniform pedestrian scale lighting, with a minimum of 30 lux; install the light poles to avoid damage to the tree root system.
Emergency waiting area	Provide a dedicated, well-lit area with an active emergency call facility.

Figure 21: Improving Safety and Security

Sources: Bangladesh Police. 2020. Emergency Hotline Numbers. Bangladesh Police, Discipline Security Progress. 2020. (accessed 5 March 2023); Asian Development Bank.

3.2.5 Provide for and improve existing amenities.

The goal is to provide and improve the quality of existing furniture and amenities to ensure that people of different age groups can use the park comfortably and conveniently. Park furniture includes benches, tables, waste bins, pavilions or pergolas, drinking fountains, and energy-efficient lighting, especially on main paths and floodlights where necessary. The following criteria should be considered when designing a public open space:

Nursing spaces

Provide segregated spaces like a room or an enclosed green space to ensure privacy for mothers to feed their infants at ease without any disturbance from strangers. The nursing space should have a chair or a couch, a small table or flat surface, a sink for washing hands or pump parts, and an electric outlet important for those who are pumping. It may also have privacy screens, a footstool as fits the needs, a visitor log, and include refreshments. Nursing spaces should not be provided in a restroom (Figure 22).

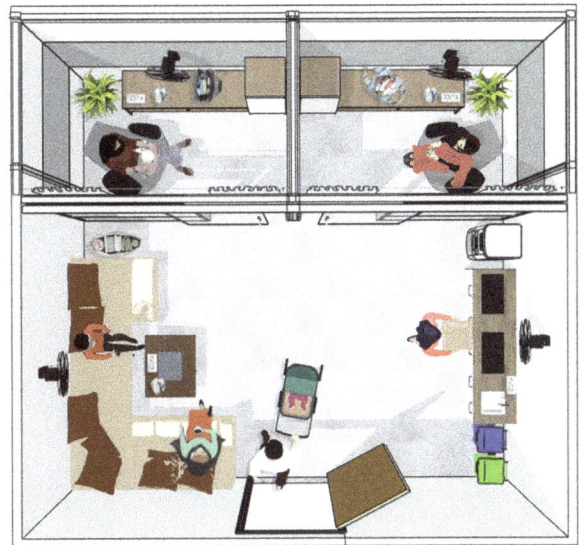

Figure 22: Nursing Room

Source: Asian Development Bank.

Provide shaded seating in public open spaces (photo by Sonal Shah, ADB [Khulna]; Sthanik Consultants, Lead Architects: Saiqa Iqbal Meghna and Suvro Sovon Chowdhury [Dhaka]).

Sitting areas

Provide different types of shaded seating or resting places at short intervals (not more than 50 meters): benches, pavilions, pergolas, and gazebos. The height can range from 450 to 500 millimeters (mm) with backrests; locate the seating in shaded areas along and away from travel paths (photo).

Seating for persons with disabilities should be at 450 to 500 mm, with a backrest and handrest at 700 mm; demarcate waiting areas for wheelchair users; provide supported swing seats with harnesses, wheelchair-accessible roundabouts, and slides that follow the ground contours.

Garbage bins

All trash receptacles should include options for dry waste and wet waste, and usable by persons with disabilities; place them adjacent to a travel path accessible to persons with disabilities, and at the exits of eating areas.

Drinking water

All drinking fountains shall be barrier-free and located near actively used areas of the public open space such as children's play areas.

Public toilets

Provide public toilets for men and women, and universally accessible, gender-neutral cubicles with commodes for children. The toilets should include western and Indian pans (or squatting pans) and consider more cubicles for women, along with water for washing and dustbins for menstruating women and girls. The access to the toilet should be directly from the outside (WBB Trust 2015), well-lit, visible, and near activity areas. They should be clean and ventilated (Figure 23).

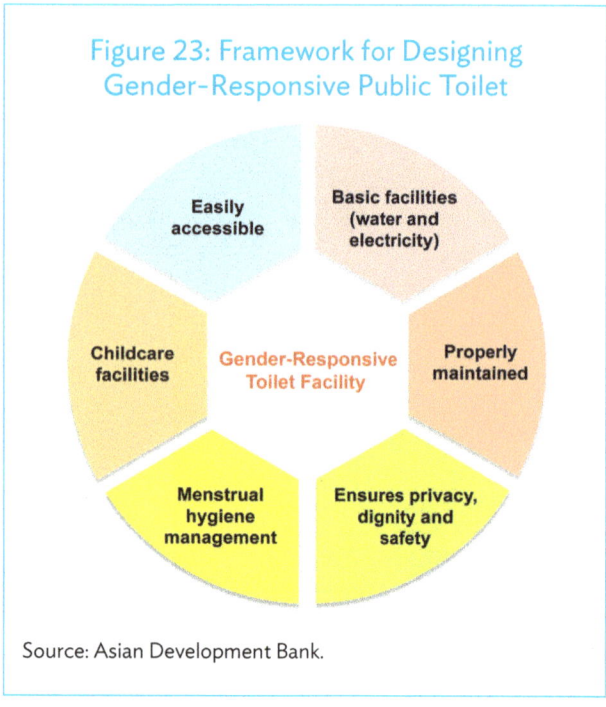

Figure 23: Framework for Designing Gender-Responsive Public Toilet

Source: Asian Development Bank.

Vending areas

Allocate spaces for stationary and mobile vendors with adequate, well-lit spaces for women (Figure 24).

Figure 24: Allocating Space for Street Vendors

Source: Asian Development Bank.

Artificial shading

Provide artificial shade to minimize heat stress from solar radiation and create a comfortable environment in a public open space. The size and kind of structure should be of human scale, to create a sense of security.

3.2.6 Placemaking

The aim is to improve the sensory experience of the open space by using contextually relevant architectural elements, materials, and signages that become an identity for the public open space.

Streets, parks, playgrounds, gardens, tot lots

Architectural Elements	
Visual elements	Draw people into and through the space with visual elements such as a large tree, sculpture, or performance space (photo).
Sensory experience	Select local plants and landscape elements that are harmonized with the design and engage the senses. For example, a running-water feature, including bright varieties of fish and water plants in ponds.
Art	Include locally relevant urban art and encourage underrepresented artists.

Open-air theater in a public open space (photo by Sthanik Consultants, Lead Architects: Saiqa Iqbal Meghna and Suvro Sovon Chowdhury).

Materials and Surfaces	
Playground surface	Soft to limit injury from falls, but firm and stable for a wheelchair user or a person using a walking aid.
Hard surfaces	Nonslip, permeable, and resin-bound (Figure 25).
Gradient	Relatively flat with a gradient of 2%–5%.

Figure 25: Using Material Suitable for All-Weather Conditions

Source: Sthanik Consultants, Lead Architects: Saiqa Iqbal Meghna and Suvro Sovon Chowdhury.

Signage system in English and Bangla	
Types of signage	Maps, directional or wayfinding, information, educational, emergency and hazard warnings
Legibility	Clear, easy to read and understand, properly lit at night, visible, and strategically located
Surfaces	Surfaces should prevent glare and be of durable weather-resistant material
Colors	Contrast with the surrounding surface to assist people with limited vision
International symbol of access	Used where appropriate (for example, in parking lots, nursing stations, and toilets for persons with disabilities)
Safety and positive gender socialization	Symbols and images to promote positive gender norms and socialization and communicate a zero-tolerance approach to sexual exploitation, abuse, and harassment (SEAH), and encourage bystander intervention.

3.2.7 Improve communication and encourage behavior change.

Prepare a detailed plan in collaboration with civil society organizations to prevent gender-based violence (GBV), and improve access to information:

- Symbols and images to break gender stereotypes and promote positive gender norms and socialization.
- Zero-tolerance approach to SEAH and encourage bystander intervention.
- Encourage women, girls, and gender minorities to report.
- Improve information on helplines and service providers for GBV and SEAH.
- Engage men and boys on preventing GBV and SEAH.

Design brief for public open spaces in Bagerhat and Kuakata in Bangladesh are created based on the abovementioned design strategies (Figure 26, Appendix 3-3, 3-4).

Figure 26: Barisal–Patuakhali Road in Kuakata

Before

After

Source: Asian Development Bank.

3.3 Test On-Site and Obtain Feedback

Tactical trials help test the design through low-cost interventions over a short period of time (7 to 15 days). This helps in course correction by assessing user responses (Figure 27).

- **Obtain permission** from the concerned authorities (such as the landowning agency and the traffic police) to implement the trial.
- **Find an appropriate period (minimum of 1 week)**, detail the proposed time-based activities, and communicate the intent to the community and stakeholders. The trial could include
  o   play equipment to engage children;
  o   canvas or water-resistant materials for shade;
  o   plow grass surfaces;
  o   access ramps to make walkways and entrances accessible; upgrade public toilets, where they exist;
  o   temporary, private nursing spaces; and
  o   for streets, use cones, and paint planters to create safe pedestrian and cycling facilities and intersections.

The material must be locally available and low-cost, which may include paint, bamboo, tires, textile, traffic barriers, and safety chains.

- **Plan activities to engage different groups**
  o   Multiple activities should be conducted to help the user reimagine one public space for different uses and activities. These include meditation camps, children's play activities, games, art competitions, and plant distribution nurseries.
  o   Organize events to involve underrepresented users such as teaching women and girls how to cycle, street art, plays, music performances, and games.
  o   Behavior-change messages can be displayed, and workshops conducted to increase awareness on GBV, sociocultural and gender norms, stereotypes, and positive gender socialization.
  o   Three-dimensional or 3D drawings of the proposed design can be displayed to create awareness.
- **Prepare an implementation schedule**
  o   A schedule should be created for a 1-week-long pilot testing. It should clearly indicate the timeline for preparing the site for the trial (Table 7).

Figure 27: Tactical Trial at Sector 2 Market, Rohtak

Source: Advait Jani, WRI India, 2023.

Table 7: Implementation Schedule for 1-Week-Long Pilot Testing

Indicators	Time of Day	Time for Preparing the Site (days)
Streets and pathways	Night	Day 1: Setting up the cones, and basic road markings Day 2 and 3: Placemaking through attractive art on the road
Pocket, neighborhood, district, and regional public open space	Day	Day 1: Pots, tires, canvas cloth, and other found material on-site
Market	Night	Day 1: Pots, tires, canvas cloth, and other found material on-site

- **Measure the response**
  - o The impact should be measured with indicators that measure an improvement in the perception of safety, comfort, and convenience by gender, age, and abilities (Table 8).[6]

Table 8: Indicators to Assess Impact of the Trial

Indicators	Performance Measure
Increase in the number of previously underrepresented groups	Increase in the number of women, girls, and persons with disabilities using the public open space
Quality of experience	Improvement in the safety, comfort, and convenience for users, of different ages, genders, and abilities
Quality of amenities (Can be considered)	Improvement in the location of street furniture, well-lit spaces, accessible public infrastructure, well-equipped play areas, and outdoor gym equipment

  - o The use of public open space, people's perceptions, and experiences should be captured using notes, photographs, videos, and drone images. The space needs to be documented at multiple times of the day, especially during specific events.
  - o The data on several underrepresented users can be collected on the third or fourth day after some stabilization is achieved.
  - o Additionally, more interested volunteers and advocacy groups can be identified during the exercise to help maintain the space and engage during the permanent construction of the project.

If a tactical trial is not conducted, a multistakeholder workshop or town hall can be organized along with obtaining inputs through the website or on-site exhibition over a weekend. The concept plan can be revised based on the tactical trial. The plan, 3D views, and report can be presented to the advisory group for approval (Figure 28).

Figure 28: Concept Design of a Pedestrianized Street in Kuakata

Source: Asian Development Bank.

---

[6] Women's and men's experience and perception of safety are different and may be determined by different causes. Women and girls are more likely to face sexual abuse and harassment, whereas men's safety may be threatened by bullying or theft.

Jessore Pouro Park, Bangladesh. Students in Jessore Pouro Park (photo by Sonal Shah, ADB).

Implement

This section provides guidance on preparing the project proposal and different models of implementation including community-based financing, contracting, and volunteering. The implementation modality is to be planned from the inception stage to link it with the different project stages and documents.

4.1 Prepare the Project Proposal

The technical team will prepare the project proposal, which includes the design and cost estimation, and is used to obtain internal approval from concerned authorities. If required, a Development Project Proposal following the format of the Planning Commission can be prepared for obtaining approvals.[7] Sustainable materials and products should be included in the specifications and incorporated into the schedule of rates. In general, the *pourashavas* will lead the procurement, but the LGED may also perform this role, if the public open space subproject is being managed by the LGED.

4.2 Plan the Implementation Modality

There are different modalities for implementing a public open space project. It could be through private contractors or through community contracts (Table 9).

Table 9: Implementation Modalities and Characteristics

Implementation Mode	Characteristics
Contractor	The contractor implements the project. Goods and services could be procured from organizations with women and other genders in founding or partnership roles (photo).
Community (Community contract)	Community groups such as self-help groups are employed.

Source: Authors.

Involve women in managerial positions. City Region Development Project 2, Local Government Engineering Department.

---

[7] Government of the People's Republic of Bangladesh, Planning Commission. DPP format. https://plandiv.gov.bd/site/forms/22f6c24f-0cc5-40d8-9874-bc9277c68643/%E0%A6%A1%E0%A6%BF%E0%A6%AA%E0%A6%BF%E0%A6%AA%E0%A6%BF-%E0%A6%9B%E0%A6%95.

4.3 Prepare the Tender Documents

The tender documents include the detailed design, working drawings, specifications, cost estimation, and conditions of the contract. It is important to assess and incorporate sustainable maintenance into the Statement of Requirements and consider 3–5 years of maintenance[8] after implementation in the conditions of the contract, instead of the existing 1-year defect liability period. To enable this, a program-based approach may be more suitable than a project-based approach.

The LGED's procurement is guided by the Public Procurement Act, 2006 and rules. Currently, it does not have a provision for gender-responsive procurement. While amending the rules may facilitate this in the long term, in the short term, smaller contracts may be considered to encourage women, gender minority, and persons with disabilities. The Gender Forum can also maintain a database and network of entrepreneurs across the country and make it available to the *pourashavas*.

Gender-responsive procurement of goods and services can be initiated to encourage organizations with women in founding or partnership roles. Plants, saplings, and vegetation may be procured from nurseries owned by women and persons with disabilities. Furthermore, women should be employed in the construction works, and in managerial and leadership positions. Training should be provided in working with sustainable materials and products (ADB 2022b).

Social and environmental safeguard documents should also be included. This involves providing access to safe, accessible, affordable housing for households headed by women, men, and families close to the public open space under construction. It also includes access to hygienic and gender-segregated public toilets, on-site creches, ensuring workplace safety, instituting a grievance redress mechanism, and sensitization on SEAH.

4.4 Manage Construction Activities

Construction management is the responsibility of the project management team, which requires contract administration and quality control of civil works. Due diligence is to review how the contractor is implementing the specific design features and construction process, quality control measures, gender considerations, and social and environmental safeguards.

Design features and measures for gender and social inclusion, climate resiliency, and environmental sustainability should be given priority during the due-diligence activities, and the contractor must be aware of them. The gender equality expert in the technical team could support the project management team.

---

[8] This is implemented in the Rural Transport Improvement Project, undertaken by the LGED.

Rakhain Market. A market run by small ethnic community in Mistrypara, Bangladesh (photo by Sonal Shah, ADB).

Manage

5.1 Identify Maintenance Funding Sources

Maintenance is an essential element of quality public open spaces. Maintenance relates to the day-to-day management of public open space assets. In small and medium-sized towns in Bangladesh, lack of funds is a major obstacle to improving and maintaining the quality of public open spaces. Finances are required for one-off improvements, renovations, and equipment, and for maintenance and staffing. Other factors for the declining quality of public open spaces are a lack of political commitment, an overall strategy, a modern management regime, and updated information on the public open space.

Conventional maintenance funding sources for public open spaces are budgetary allocations; grants from the central government; user fees; revenues from private sources in lieu of advertisements; operating businesses such as restaurants or cafés; and some other sources like philanthropy or crowdsourcing, earmarked off-site revenues, and in-kind contributions.

5.2 Develop an Operation and Maintenance Plan

Local authorities are predominantly responsible for the management of public open spaces, which requires active collaboration among residents, civil society, and the private sector (INU 2016). The *pourashavas* should develop operational plans for its public open spaces in consultation with the working group.

Operations of public open spaces require the daily management of the physical space, encompassing cleaning, beautification, visitor movement control, infrastructure maintenance, landscaping and gardening, parking, and allocation of spaces and facilities for tenants and vendors.

5.2.1 Develop a suitable maintenance model

Effective maintenance of public open spaces requires a strategic perspective, management scheme, capacity, funding, political commitment, and public participation (Table 10).

Table 10: Elements of a Maintenance Model

Elements	Description
Strategic perspective	A clear understanding of the maintenance requirements of the public open space, which is incorporated in the project design and implementation. This also includes adopting optimal design strategies and using materials with low maintenance requirements.
Management scheme	This includes outlining what needs to be maintained at what frequency, clear service-level benchmarks, and regular supervision.
Funding	A consistent source of funds is required to maintain the public open space. This includes the cost of services (such as guards and workers) and goods (such as materials and equipment).
Information and public participation	Inculcating a culture of respect in the use of the public open space and crowd-sourcing feedback from the users to maintain quality.
Capacity within the *pourashavas*	The *pourashavas* should have the capacity to create suitable contracts with the private sector and dedicated personnel for monitoring the maintenance of the public open space.

Source: Authors.

The maintenance of public open spaces is usually the responsibility of the *pourashavas*. Other arrangements can be made with the private sector and community partners. Women should be included in the supervision of maintenance activities to assess and respond to the needs of women. Potential models are presented based on primary responsibility (Table 11, photo):

- City agency (*pourashavas*): This is the most common model, in which the city itself takes responsibility for maintenance.
- Private sector: Contractors can be hired by the city (*pourashavas*) specifically for public space maintenance or maintain it in lieu of revenue generation.
- Partnership and community stewardship: Locally organized groups form partnerships with city agencies and may be involved in the design and implementation process. This includes business and residents' associations, sports clubs, among

A well-maintained public open space in Bangladesh (photo by Sonal Shah, ADB).

Table 11: Different Models for Maintenance of Public Open Spaces in Bangladesh

Responsible entity	Organizational Structure			Stakeholders	Pros and Cons
	Funding	Maintenance	Monitoring		
City agency (*pourashavas*)	*Pourashavas* and government	*Pourashavas*	*Pourashavas* and users	T1, T2, T3	• Pros: Better control and consistency. • Cons: If the *pourashavas* does not have sustained funding and capacity, it can result in public open space being neglected.
Private sector	*Pourashavas* and government	Private sector	*Pourashavas* and users	T1, T2, T3	• Pros: Reduced workload for the *pourashavas*. • Cons: Requires sustained funding, a clear management scheme with service-level benchmarks, and regular monitoring.
Private sector	Private sector/ nongovernment organizations	Private sector	*Pourashavas* and users	T1, T3	• Pros: Reduced cost for the *pourashavas*. • Cons: Requires a management scheme with the service-level benchmarks and regular monitoring by the *pourashavas*.
Partnership and community stewardship	*Pourashavas* and government	*Pourashavas* and community	*Pourashavas*, community, and users	T1, T2, T3	• Pros: Reduced workload and cost for the *pourashavas*. • Cons: Requires community mobilization, consistent support, and clear identification of roles and responsibilities.
Multi-agency	*Pourashavas* and government	*Pourashavas* and other agencies (e.g., corporate sector)	*Pourashavas* and users	T1, T3	• Pros: Reduced cost of the *pourashavas*. • Cons: Requires clear service-level benchmarks and monitoring by the *pourashavas*.

Tn = tier 1, 2, or 3.
Source: Authors.

others. Users may contribute to maintenance by reporting the specific maintenance needs. Where feasible, use materials, products, and equipment that are readily available and accessible (i.e., materials, parts, and tools).
- Multi-agency responsibility: Multiple agencies share responsibility for the maintenance of the park, toilet, and other facilities or elements.

5.3 Create a Monitoring and Evaluation Plan

Regular monitoring is essential to ensure the usability of public open spaces. Successful monitoring processes require reliable and adequate information on public open spaces. Major monitoring information requirements are as follows:

- The condition of the public open space is measured through user satisfaction levels, an inventory of all the street furniture, amenities, landscaped areas, and water bodies with regular monitoring. Feedback on the conditions of existing facilities can be obtained through numerous channels such as phone calls or messages, social media, and on-site feedback boxes.
- Schedule and prioritize maintenance based on an urgent, regular, and periodic basis (Appendix 5-1).
- Resources, staff, and equipment required and used.
- Expenditure incurred for maintenance of the public open space.
- Maintenance problems encountered.

Case example: Pouro Park, Jessore

The Jessore *pourashavas* has developed a 12-acre Pouro Park, adjacent to its office and a school. It includes a lake, walkways, and small play areas for children. It has provided a designated area for women, along with an art center to organize activities in the park. There is a gender-segregated public toilet, with a (steep) ramp. The capital investments were done through several projects, such as the Second City Region Development Project (CRDP 2) and the Third Urban Governance and Infrastructure Improvement (Sector) Project (UGIIP-3)[9] (Figure 29).

The *pourashavas* allocates funds from its own source for maintaining the Pouro Park. The monthly maintenance cost is around Taka (Tk) 150,000, and an annual budget is allocated for park maintenance. While there are no entrance fees, Tk10 is charged as user fee for using the public toilet.

The *pourashavas* has assigned two officials—one from the engineering department and one from the conservancy department—to supervise maintenance activities. This is an example of a city agency (*pourashavas*) maintenance model without a formal committee. There are suggestion boxes at the entrance of the park and at the *pourashavas* office to obtain feedback from park users. According to the *pourashavas*, supervisors visit the park periodically and CCTVs are installed to monitor activities.

Figure 29: Continuous Walkway Along the Lake Edge in Jessore Pouro Park

Source: Sonal Shah, Asian Development Bank.

---

[9] ADB. Bangladesh : Second City Region Development Project; Government of Bangladesh, LGED. Third Urban Governance and Infrastructure Improvement (Sector) Project (UGIIP-III) (UGIIP-3).

A water channel in Khulna University (photo by Sonal Shah, ADB).

Conclusion

Culture and climate differ all over the world, but people are the same. They'll gather in public if you give them a good place to do it.
-Jan Gehl

When planners fail to account for gender, public space become [sic] male spaces by default.
-Caroline Criado-Perez

Public open spaces are an integral part of our everyday urban life. They are all around us; the streets we walk on, places where children play, where we can encounter nature. In coastal towns of Bangladesh, they can play a crucial role in climate adaptation. This guideline aims to provide the tools to create a climate-resilient public realm that residents enjoy, especially those who are currently underrepresented: women, gender minorities, girls, and persons with disabilities.

Women sitting along the lake edge. A public open space in Jessore, Bangladesh (photo by Sonal Shah).

Appendixes

Introduction

Appendix 1-1: Checklist outlining the tools for public open space selection, development, and management

Process	Tools	References	Outputs and Outcomes
Stage 1: Prioritize and Prepare			
1.1 Constitute a preliminary team	Section 1.1		Preliminary team
1.2 Prioritize and select a public open space	Stakeholder map	Figure 6	Inventory of at least three public open spaces
	Scoring matrix for prioritizing the public open space	Appendix 1-2	
FOR CONSIDERATION: Constitute a public open space working group	Working group members	Box 1	Public open space working group
1.3 Assess and strengthen the capacity of the *pourashavas*	Different team structure	pp. 7–8	Existing and required resources
1.4 Prepare a communication and outreach strategy	Stakeholder analysis table for selected public open space	Appendix 1-3	Work plan, outputs for different stages, outreach and communications strategy
	Communication methods	Appendix 1-4	
	Stages, outputs, and indicative communication methods	Table 3	
1.5 Prepare a base map and conduct a reconnaissance survey	Base map	Figure 9	Base map
	Total station survey	Appendix 1-5	
Stage 2: Assess			
	Matrix of climate risks	Table 4	
2.1 Assess the local blue–green–gray network and impact of climate risks on the public open space	Data sources	Appendix 2-1	Information on regional and site-specific natural and physical features and climate risk
2.2 Conduct a detailed assessment of the public open space	Stakeholder engagement tools • User surveys • Focus group discussion questions • Key informant interview questions • Occasional, rare, and non-user surveys	Appendix 2-2 Appendix 2-3 Appendix 2-4 Appendix 2-5 Appendix 2-6	Assessment of existing climate risks, user and non-user perspectives, barriers and expectations Existing natural and physical features of the site and its influence area, existing space usage, amenities and infrastructure, safety and accessibility situation of the selected public open space

continued on next page

Appendixes *continued*

Process	Tools	References	Outputs and outcomes
	Design Criteria • Local blue–green–gray networks and climate risks • Connectivity and access • Layout, activities, and use • Climate adaptation interventions • Safety and security • Street furniture and amenities • Universal design • Placemaking • Information and communications • Events	Figure 11, Table 4, Appendix 2-1 Figure 12 Figure 13, Figure 14, Appendix 2-7 Figure 15 Figure 16 Figure 17, p. 18 pp. 18–19, Appendix 3 p. 19 p. 19 p. 19	
2.3 Conduct participatory safety audit	Safety audit checklist and methodology	Appendix 2-9	
2.4 Conduct participatory accessibility audit	Accessibility audit checklist and methodology	Appendix 2-10	
2.5 Understand the barriers and expectations of diverse groups	On-site exhibition, design charrette, and visioning workshop	Appendix 2-11	
Stage 3: Create			
3.1 Facilitate a multistakeholder visioning workshop	Design charrette, visioning workshop	Appendix 3-1	Participatory envisioning of the public open space, outline design priorities and amenities
3.2 Create a concept plan	Design criteria • Climate adaptation • Connectivity and access • Layout • Safety and security • Street furniture and amenities • Placemaking • Information and communications • Universal accessibility • Design briefs for Barishal–Pathuakali Road • Design brief for Rupa Chaudhary Pouro Park	Figures 21, 22, Table 5 p. 29, Figure 23 pp. 30–31, Table 6, Figures 24, 25 p. 32, Figure 26 pp. 32–34 pp. 34–35 p. 35 Appendix 3-2 Appendix 3-3 Appendix 3-4	Translate priorities into design strategies and prepare a concept plan
3.3 Test on-site and obtain feedback	Trials Multistakeholder validation workshop	pp. 36–37 p. 37	Test the design, observe impact, and revise the concept plan
Stage 4: Implement			
4.1 Prepare the project proposal		p. 39	Detailed architectural, engineering landscape design drawings Working drawings Specifications, bill of quantities and cost estimation Development Project Proposal, if required
4.2 Plan the implementation modality	Different implementation models	Table 9	Implementation modality, roles, and schedule
4.3 Preparing tender documents		p. 40	Tender documents with gender inclusive procurement, sustainable materials, and maintenance period

continued on next page

Appendixes continued

Process	Tools	References	Outputs and outcomes
4.4 Manage construction activities		p. 40	Project management, quality control, gender considerations, social and environment safeguards
Stage 5: Manage			
5.1 Identify maintenance funding source		p. 42	
5.2 Develop an Operation and Maintenance Plan	Maintenance models	Table 10, Table 11	Operations and maintenance plan
5.3 Create a monitoring and evaluation plan	Type and schedule of maintenance	Appendix 5-1	Monitoring plan

Source: Authors.

Appendix 1: Prepare and Prioritize

Appendix 1-2: Criteria for prioritizing the public open space

Selection of the Ward	Indicator	How to Assess
Community need	Per capita public open space of the ward is less than the city average, and is the lowest among all wards	Divide the public open space at the city and/or ward level by the population of the city and/or ward

	Comparative Assessment of Public Open Spaces within a Ward				
SNo	Principles and Indicators	Score=1	Score = 0	How to Assess	Score with Justification
A	**Connectivity**				
1	Transport connectivity	Well-connected by frequent public transport and paratransit	Not well connected by frequent public transport and paratransit	Bus stop with a headway of 10 minutes or more, or a paratransit stand within 50 meters (m)	
B	**Gender and Social Inclusion**				
2	Presence of different economically vulnerable communities or user groups	Presence of one or more informal settlements and businesses within 400 m walking distance	Presence of informal settlements and businesses beyond 400 m walking distance	Count the number of informal settlements within 400 m walking distance of the public open space	
3	Percentage of women and girls using the public open space (6 a.m.–8 p.m.)	Women, girls constitute less than 40% of all users	Women, girls constitute 40% or more of all users	Count the total number of women and girls for 15-minute intervals at early morning, morning, afternoon, evening, and night; and divide by the total number of users at these times	
4	Percentage of children (<5 years or shorter than 1 m) using the public open space (6 a.m.–8 p.m.)	Share of children constitutes less than their ward population share	Share of children constitutes more than their ward population share	Count the total number of children for 15-minute intervals at early morning, morning, afternoon, evening, and night; and divide by the total number of users at these times; compare with their ward population share	
5	Minority or indigenous groups	Ethnic minority groups are supported or not negatively impacted through the project	Ethnic minority groups are negatively impacted or relocated through the project	Key informant interviews with the representatives of ethnic minority groups	
6	Resettlement of existing users	Residents of informal settlements and businesses are supported and not harmed	Residents of informal settlements and businesses are to be relocated or evicted	Estimated number of residents and business to be relocated or evicted	
C	**Climate Vulnerability Adaptation and Environment**				
7	Public space vulnerability to climate risks such as earthquakes, tidal surges, groundwater salinity, and river floods	It is not directly affected by any of the climate risks	It is directly affected by at least one of the climate risks	Urban development reports, key informant interviews with community representatives	

continued on next page

Appendix 1-2 *continued*

	Comparative Assessment of Public Open Spaces within a Ward				
SNo	Principles and Indicators	Score=1	Score = 0	How to Assess	Score with Justification
8	Potential of the public open space to become a refuge for cyclone, flood, and earthquake	Public open space can become a refuge for all the three disasters	Public open space can become a refuge for two or less disasters	Urban development reports, key informant interviews with experts	
9	Sustainable infrastructure or nature-based solutions (NBS) application	Has the potential of demonstrating climate resilient or NBS in designing infrastructure and amenities of the public space[a]	No possibility		
D	**Landownership and Area**				
10	Landownership	*Pourashavas* or any other government agency	Nongovernment entity	Land records	
E	**Additional Parameters**				
i	Preservation or creation of livelihood opportunities	Existing livelihoods are preserved, and more opportunities can be created	Livelihoods are not created by the public open space development or are relocated	Number or livelihoods preserved or relocated, and the number of livelihoods generated	
ii	Frequency of gatherings or festivals	Weekly	Less frequent than weekly events		
iii	Cultural and social significance	Has national, district, or local cultural and social significance within 400 m walking distance	Does not have a cultural or social significance	Urban development reports, key informant interviews with experts, community members	

[a] Such as tree plantation, rain garden, rainwater harvesting, groundwater recharging, ecological water, and flood management

Note: Public open spaces with a higher score are to be prioritized. Where the scores of the public open spaces are at par, prioritize those which result in the least number of persons and businesses relocated or evicted; Support the comparative assessment with photo documentation of its physical and environmental conditions and understand the regulations affecting the design of the public open space, development history, and future proposals.

Source: Authors.

Appendix 1-3: Agenda for capacity development on urban planning, public open space development, and governance

The workshop can be organized for 20–30 participants, and the preparation will require a projector, screen, microphones, note pads, pens. If a 2-day workshop is feasible, then consider assessing a public open space along with preparing concept strategies. This will additionally require A4 or A3 print outs of the public open space along with the relevant prints of the assessment tools.

Time	Activity
10:00 a.m.–10:30 a.m.	Registration of participants
10:30 a.m.–11:00 a.m.	Introduction to the workshop objectives, agenda, and participants
11:00 a.m.–12.00 p.m.	Introduction to urban planning and governance in Bangladesh (*Interactive presentation along with participatory exercises*)
12:00 p.m.–1:15 p.m.	Lunch break

continued on next page

Appendix 1_3 continued

Time	Activity
1:15 p.m.–2:30 p.m.	Select and Prepare *(Outline the process of selecting a public open space, constituting a working group, capacity assessment and augmentation in the Pourashavas, stakeholder identification and engagement strategy)*
2:30 p.m.–4:00 p.m.	Assess, Create, Implement, and Maintain *(Assess the public open space, create and test the concept plan, prepare detail designs, cost estimation, implementation modality and maintenance models)*
4:00 p.m.–4:30 p.m.	Feedback on the workshop and concluding remarks.

Source: Authors.

Appendix 1-4: Stakeholder roles and contributions

Type of Stakeholder	Stakeholder Name	Role		Tier of Stakeholder
Central government	Urban development directorate	Enhance public open spaces	Policies, master plan, standards	T1
	Local Government Engineering Department	Support local government in governance-led urban infrastructure, gender responsiveness	Project implementation, Master Plans	T1
	Bangladesh railways	Utilize unused railway land	Land	T3
	Water development board	Utilize waterside lands	Land	T1, T3
Local government	*Pourashavas*/City corporation	Lead the public open space development process, improve public amenities and environment	Leadership, funding, iimplementation, maintenance of public open spaces, master plan implementation	T1
	City development authority	Development planning	Master Plan, programming, implementation	T1
Development partners	Asian Development Bank, World Bank, UN-Habitat, UNICEF, and others	Assist, finance urban infrastructure and services	Technical assistance and funding	T2
Civil society organizations	Work for a Better Bangladesh Trust, Action Aid and organizations working on gender development, universal accessibility	Help community and government, social development	Coordination, technical assistance, women-friendly public open spaces	T2
Local organizations	Schools, sports clubs, faith groups	Use the facilities, organize activities	Negotiation, volunteering	T2, T1
Professional groups	Institute of Architects Bangladesh, Bangladesh Institute of Planners, and others	Provide technical expertise in improvement of public open spaces and landscape, infrastructure and services	Technical advice	T2
Private sector		Publicity, social responsibility	Funding, maintenance	T4, T2

Tn = tier 1, 2, 3, or 4; UN = United Nations; UNICEF = United Nations Children's Fund.

Source: Authors.

Appendix 1-5: Communication methods to engage stakeholders

Methods	Description	Target Stakeholder	Number of Participants	What Can it Be Used for?
Key informant interviews	A structured interview with an individual who has expert information	T1, T2, T3	Individual	Initial assessment and context information, and follow-up interviews as required
In-depth interviews	A structured in-depth interview with an individual	T1, T2, T3, T4	Individual	Obtain specific perspectives with targeted groups such as pregnant women, a caregiver, and others.
Rapid knowledge, attitude, and practice survey	A structured questionnaire including closed and open-ended questions	T1, T3	Up to 10	Assessment of gender and social inclusion knowledge to design need-specific capacity development workshop
Focus group discussion	A facilitated discussion with a homogeneous group of people (defined by age, income, gender, and ability)	T1, T2	6-8	Gather information, perspectives, and opinions about the public open space from users and non-users
Participatory audits	An assessment of public open space with members of a community through a guided walk	T2	6-8	Assessment of a public open space by a specific user group (such as women, girls, other genders, and persons with disabilities) gathering physical and non-physical attributes. This can be conducted using digital tools.
Visioning workshop or a design charrette	A structured workshop aimed at developing a design or vision for a project or planning activity	T1, T2, T3, T4	30–60	Issue identification, vision, and design development.
Outdoor exhibition	A public exhibition to obtain input or disseminate information. It can be used along with surveys or visioning workshops to obtain perspectives from a wider group of people.	T2	On a rolling basis	Gather perspectives on the perception of the public open space, expectations, and participatory vision development; obtain feedback on the concept plan
Public town hall meeting	A planned meeting where a public official addresses and answers questions from members of the public	T1, T2, T3, T4	It is open to the public	Present and obtain feedback on the concept plan
Awareness raising campaigns on gender roles and universal access	A process to inform and educate people on gender inequity in the city with the objective of influencing their attitudes, behaviors, and beliefs. These can also be used to increase awareness on the difficulties faced by persons with disabilities in using public spaces.	T1, T2	City-wide and site-specific	During the pilot testing of the design, it can be done through plays, forum theater, and other events

Tn = tier 1, 2, 3, or 4.
Source: Authors.

Appendix 1-6: Scope of work for total station survey

Scope of Work

The consultant will be responsible for conducting the total station survey and preparing survey maps for the public open space.

Survey Tasks

- Topographic surveys – The survey should capture all the details on and along the survey corridor to enable three-dimensional (3D) road profiling for the creation of longitudinal and cross-profiles to be carried.

- Specific elements that must be surveyed include the following:
  1. Existing buildings or structures (indication only)
  2. Main roads, sub-roads including diversions
  3. Signals and/or road marking
  4. Junctions
  5. Roundabouts
  6. Medians, bollards, permanent barricades
  7. Compound walls
  8. All utility (ducts and/or pipelines electricity, telephone, stormwater, sewer, lighting, gas, oil pipeline, and others) poles and/or boxes
  9. Overhead high-tension lines
  10. Trees: to be indicated in two categories, above and below 30 centimeters of main trunk circumference
  11. Footpaths, pathways, platforms, sidewalks, and others with all the features
  12. Kerbs
  13. Manholes
  14. Pedestrian crossings
  15. Drains (covered and uncovered)
  16. Signboards and/or markings should also cover a survey of existing safety signages, directional signages, and others
  17. Service lines and/or cable ducts
  18. Difference in levels wherever it occurs
  19. Establishing true and/or magnetic north point with respect to each location
  20. Establishing reduced and/or relative level for each item and/or turn
  21. Location, name and size of trees, marking shrub areas and current condition of trees.
  22. Location of temporary structures like sheds or informal structures and their purpose.
  23. Demarcation of the slum, market, industry, and others adjacent to the street
  24. Location of skywalks and/or foot over the bridge, if any

- The width of the road survey shall cover compound wall to compound wall showing the access of each property. If there are crossroads, then 100 meters (m) or until the end of the first few property boundaries along the perpendicular streets that connect to the main road that is being surveyed.

- In case of major crossroads, up to 100 m shall be surveyed. In the case of minor crossroads, only a depth up to 50 m shall be surveyed. Detailed study of flyover both top and bottom, including ascending and descending points, pillar positions, varying widths and heights, grid levels, handrail and/or barricading detail, lampposts, service lines, structural dimensions of the flyover, any structure underneath the flyover, and others.

- All survey work is to be checked and approved by architects and any remaining data set shall be arranged for before completion and the full payments are eligible only on the full satisfaction of the architect.

Final Survey Drawing Requirements

- The survey drawings must be on true north, with the correct global positioning system (GPS) location on the AutoCAD drawing. A minimum of three benchmark points must be given for each individual street for cross-checking coordinates at the site.

- The survey shall be taken beyond the right-of-way for the connecting streets all along the proposed corridor with footprints of buildings or 50 m (whichever is less) on both sides of the corridor and connecting streets showing entry, exit points, gates, and others.

- To carry out parking (off-street and on-street) and activity survey along the corridor.

- Vending activities and cycle docking stations should be mapped, if any.

- Detailed road inventory study. Study of existing openings in central verge and/or intersection, side footpath, and others.

continued on next page

Appendixes 1–6 *continued*

Final Survey Drawing Requirements
• Surveyor should also collect data on infrastructure existing on the ground, below and above the ground, and levels of the ground and identify the monument, reserved green and or parks, and sensitive or defence areas in the vicinity and their influence on the proposed corridor. To obtain details of underground or over-ground services from various utility departments like *pourashavas*, subzonal office, Bangladesh Telecommunications Company Limited, Water Development Board, and others.
• Locations of trees with girth (measured at 1 m height from the ground level) in separate AutoCad layers. A table, showing the location, type species and girth diameter, and reference number duly shown on the plan shall be made. The trees at the site are to be numbered and marked with paint including the identification of trees, which can be saved (without cutting) if falling on the median.
• Benchmark to be clearly marked so that during construction it can be located.
• Provide chainage and cross-sections every 50 m.
• Basic levels of the road at every chainage.
• Footpath level to be given at every chainage or if a sudden change in level occurs at certain places.
• Provide drain locations, invert levels, light pole locations, feeder pillars, paving details, existing transformers, and existing constructions (if any).
• Property names adjacent to the corridor and junction.

Source: Authors.

Appendix 2: Assess

Appendix 2-1: Data source and methodology for assessment at the metropolitan, precinct, and site scales

Assessment	Objective	Data Source and Methodology
Average minimum and maximum temperature	Map the maximum and minimum temperature, aberration, and its duration in the region or city.	• Bangladesh Meteorological Department • Atkins and ADB – Lessons learned from Second Coastal Towns Environmental Infrastructure Improvement Sector Project (SCTEIIP) Phase 1, 2020
Annual and peak rainfall	Assess the aberration, annual and peak rainfall, and its duration in the region or city during peak rainfall	• Bangladesh Meteorological Department • Atkins and ADB – Lessons learned from SCTEIIP Phase 1, 2020
Land cover	Assess the land area distribution of a district and area under land, reserve forest, and riverine area; developed and undeveloped area	• Global information system (GIS) Shapefiles from Ministry of Land • Bangladesh Disaster-Prone Area Atlas for respective Zila, 2021
Sea level rise projection	Map the High Tide Line and Low Tide Line to define areas at risk of inundation, storm surges, erosion, and possible soil contamination	• Master plan report
Tidal bore-prone area	To assess the high and low-lying affected areas from the tidal waves in the precinct or site.	• Master plan report
Flood-prone area	To assess the high and low-lying affected areas at the regional, city and precinct levels	• Master plan report • Atkins and ADB – Lessons learned from SCTEIIP Phase 1 2020 • Bangladesh Disaster-Prone Area Atlas for respective Zila, 2021 • Digital elevation model (DEM) using slope and hydrology, rainfall data using GIS analysis.
Watershed	Map the terrain topography of the region/city from where the water runoff is drained to the outflow of a reservoir, the mouth of a bay, or any point along a stream channel	• GIS analysis from DEM data-slope, hydrology, and land cover data
Cyclone-prone area	Use a 25–100-year cyclone map to define high-risk areas for prudent infrastructure planning and site selection	• Atkins and ADB – Lessons learned from Coastal Town Environmental Improvement Investment Program Phase 1, 2020
Embankment erosion	To determine the rate of riverbank erosion at the metropolitan, precinct and site levels	• Satellite imagery from remote sensing and GIS analysis
Salinity intrusion and other contaminations	Determine the level of saline intrusion to assess possible damage to the land	• Point-based GIS Shapefiles from Bangladesh Agricultural Research Council • Centre for Environmental and Geographic Information Services • Site soil analysis
Blue-green cover network	To map the green public open space network of playgrounds, parks, institutional land, and agricultural fields at the precinct level and if relevant at the city level	• Master Plan • Satellite images
Stormwater network	Map the water runoff network of the city to assess the existing drainage system.	• DEM using GIS analysis • GIS data from *pourashavas* • Master plan report

continued on next page

Appendix 2-1 *continued*

Assessment	Objective	Data Source and Methodology
Waterlogged area	Map the catchment areas in the city and the precinct caused by rain, runoff, interflow, rise in groundwater, over-irrigation, or flooding.	• DEM using GIS analysis • GIS data from *Pourashavas*
Micro-watershed	Map the terrain topography from where the water runoff is drained to the outflow of a reservoir, the mouth of a bay, or any point along a stream channel.	• DEM data-slope and hydrology, rainfall data, and land cover data using GIS analysis
Slope analysis	To determine the topography of the site to assess the drainage or the water flow.	• DEM using GIS analysis
Soil quality	To assess soil type, condition, salinity, bearing capacity, porosity, and absorption for infrastructure planning (built, green, and gray)	• Soil test to be conducted at a minimum of two locations depending on the context during primary data collection
Vegetation inventory	To map the type of trees, shrubs, crops for farming, and other plantations in the precinct.	• A survey conducted during the reconnaissance survey
Aquifer zone	Map the favorable aquifer zone for recharge of groundwater. *Additional analysis at the precinct and site scales*	• Field investigations and DEM using GIS analysis

Source: Authors.

Appendix 2-2: Stakeholder engagement

SNo	Tool	Materials	Planned Activity	Time Allocation
1	User and non-user surveys	• Survey forms, pens • Folders to organize the forms • For the user survey questionnaire, refer to Appendix 2-4 • For the non-user survey questionnaire, refer to Appendix 2-7	• Identify locations at the public open space • Approach every third person passing by the designated area • If too crowded, approach every fifth person • Clearly mention the aim and expected outcome of this exercise • Stay sensitive to local customs, culture • Responses remain anonymous, forms filled out by the participants	• <10 minutes for each participant • Number of surveyors will depend on the sample size
2	Focus Group Discussion (FGD) (face-to-face)	• Questionnaire, notepad, and pen; a facilitator and a note taker • Room for 8–10 seated participants • Ensure gender balance in the participants • A printed transcript of the agenda of the discussion • Snacks • For the questionnaire, refer to Appendix 2-5	• Facilitator clearly shares the agenda, expected outcome from this exercise, ensures consent of the participants • A guided discussion with a prepared checklist and indicative questions • Facilitator will conduct the discussion with participants ensuring everyone is meaningfully engaged, and comfortable	• 2–3 hours session with each group of women, girls, other genders, and persons with disabilities

continued on next page

Appendix 2-2 *continued*

SNo	Tool	Materials	Planned Activity	Time Allocation
		• For FGDs with persons with a disability, ensure there are two sign language interpreters	• All discussions are documented • Ends with a vote of thanks	
3	Key Informant Interviews	• Printed questionnaires • Pen and paper • One facilitator • One person for note taking and photograph • For the questionnaire, refer to Appendix 2-6	• Rapport-building exercise should be participatory • Clearly mention the aim and expected outcome of this exercise • Stay sensitive to local customs, culture, and ensure confidentiality of identities and responses • Up to 15 responses can be collected from the mixed group of stakeholders in each district	• 2 hours • 30 minutes for introduction and rapport building

Source: Authors.

Appendix 2-3: User survey

1. Age (If below 18 years, the survey should be filled in the presence of an adult caregiver)
   - ☐ <10
   - ☐ 10–19
   - ☐ 20–29
   - ☐ 30–39
   - ☐ 40–49
   - ☐ 50+

2. Gender
   - ☐ Female
   - ☐ Male
   - ☐ Others
   - ☐ Prefer not to say

3. What best describes your relationship with this area? (Check all that apply)
   - ☐ Resident
   - ☐ Employee (of nearby institution/ office/ workers/self-employed)
   - ☐ Student (nearby school)
   - ☐ Tourist
   - ☐ Attendee (cultural event or institution)
   - ☐ Other (Please describe)

4. How often do you visit the place?
   - ☐ 6–7 days per week
   - ☐ 2–5 days per week
   - ☐ Once a week
   - ☐ Occasionally (2–3 times a month)
   - ☐ Rarely (Less than once a month)
   - ☐ First time here

5. Whom are you visiting the place with?
   - ☐ Family
   - ☐ Partner
   - ☐ Dependent
   - ☐ Friends
   - ☐ Solo

6. How did you get here today? (Select an option travelled for the longest distance)
   - ☐ Walk
   - ☐ Bicycle
   - ☐ Cycle Rickshaw
   - ☐ Easy Bike
   - ☐ Bus
   - ☐ Van
   - ☐ E-rickshaw
   - ☐ Taxi/ Rideshare
   - ☐ Private Car
   - ☐ Other (Please describe)

continued on next page

Appendix 2_3 *continued*

7. What brings you to this space?
   - ☐ Passing through
   - ☐ For purchases
   - ☐ Spend time with my family
   - ☐ Accompany my child
   - ☐ Meeting with friends
   - ☐ Spending time by myself
   - ☐ Sightseeing
   - ☐ Recreation/ Sports/ Exercise/ Playing
   - ☐ Cultural Event/ Performance
   - ☐ Political Event/ Protest
   - ☐ Others (Please describe)

8. If you answered 'just passing through' are you headed anywhere in particular?
   - ☐ Home
   - ☐ Work
   - ☐ School
   - ☐ Market
   - ☐ Restaurant/ Tea Stall/ Food Truck
   - ☐ Cultural Institution
   - ☐ Other (Please describe)

9. How much time do you plan on spending here today?
   - Less than 20 minutes
   - 20–40 minutes
   - 40–60 minutes
   - 1 hour or more

10. How do you feel about this public space?
    - ☐ Strongly negative
    - ☐ Somewhat negative
    - ☐ Somewhat positive
    - ☐ Strongly positive

11. Which three words would you use to describe this public open space?

    _____

12. Which two things would you like to do in this public space that you cannot do now?

    _____

13. What are the sounds that you associate with this public open space?

    _____

14. What are the smells or fragrances that you associate with this public open space?

    _____

15. Have you faced sexual abuse and harassment in the public open space in the last 6 months?
    - ☐ Yes
    - ☐ No

16. If yes, what type of sexual exploitation, abuse, and harassment (SEAH) did you face?
    - ☐ Staring
    - ☐ Eve teasing
    - ☐ Stalking
    - ☐ Groping
    - ☐ Others

17. How did you address it?
    - ☐ Ignored it and moved away
    - ☐ Accosted the perpetrator
    - ☐ Requested help from other users
    - ☐ Reported it to the police
    - ☐ Others

18. How has it affected your experience and access to the public open space?
    - ☐ It has not affected my access
    - ☐ I visit less often
    - ☐ I come here with a male companion
    - ☐ I come here with a female companion
    - ☐ Others

Source: Authors.
Adapted from https://issuu.com/gehlarchitects/docs/public_life_diversity_toolkit_v2_fo.

Appendix 2-4: Questionnaire for the focus group discussion

This can be conducted in a shaded area of the public open space or in the *pourashavas* office. The poll questions aim to assess the attitudes and knowledge of civil society organizations on gender roles and access to public spaces.

Poll questions

1. Which of these are public spaces from your perspective? (Select all that apply)
   a. Street
   b. Bazaar
   c. Park
   d. Playgrounds
   e. Cyclone shelters
   f. Others (Please mention)

2. Why do you think public spaces are important for women and girls?
   a. Public spaces encourage women and girls to step out of the house, unnecessarily
   b. Provide recreation and leisure
   c. Increase livelihood options
   d. Encourage active participation in sports, overall health and well-being
   e. Others (Please mention)

3. What restricts women and girls' access to public spaces in Bangladesh?
   a. Women are not restricted in accessing public spaces
   b. Safe access to public spaces
   c. Social and cultural norms
   d. Sexual exploitation, abuse, and harassment (SEAH) and lack of safety
   e. Lack of amenities such as public toilets, seating areas, and others.
   f. Others (Please mention)

4. What are the safety-related concerns for women and girls in public spaces?
   a. Road crashes
   b. Secure access at night
   c. Dark and unlit public spaces
   d. Few persons, mostly men in public spaces
   e. Sexual abuse and harassment
   f. Fear of crime
   g. Accidents due to disasters
   h. Others (Please mention)

5. What are the reasons for sexual abuse and harassment against women in public spaces?
   a. Not applicable for Bangladesh
   b. Lack of awareness of what constitutes sexual abuse and harassment
   c. Limited enforcement of law
   d. Patriarchal gender roles and perceptions
   e. Women's behavior and appearance
   f. Women's presence in public spaces after sunset
   g. Others (Please mention)

6. What are the biggest challenges for persons with disabilities in public spaces?
   a. Access to the public space
   b. Accessible infrastructure and amenities
   c. Lack of support or help from users
   d. Lack of support or help from duty bearers
   e. Limited or no information on accessible features in public spaces
   f. Others (Please mention)

7. Which of these amenities are required to encourage gender diversity in public spaces?
   a. Public toilets for all genders
   b. Private nursing spaces
   c. Play and exercise equipment for women and girls
   d. Dedicated play areas for women and girls
   e. Others (Please mention)

8. How can men and boys be engaged in preventing gender-based violence (GBV), sexual abuse and harassment in public spaces
   a. Sensitize them on GBV, women's experience of safety, sexual abuse, and harassment

continued on next page

Appendix 2-4 *continued*

    b. Increase awareness of anti-sexual harassment laws
    c. Increase awareness of positive masculinity and role models
    d. It is more important to engage women and girls than to focus on men
    e. Others (Please mention)

9. How can we create gender-responsive public spaces?
    a. Public toilets for all genders, with universal access
    b. Sensitizing society on gender diversity
    c. It is not necessary to address gender diversity in public space design
    d. Increase awareness of existing laws on third gender
    e. Highlight positive role models from gender-minority communities
    f. Others (Please mention)

Open-ended questions

1. How safe are public spaces in the city for women and girls of all ages and what are the main reasons for this?
2. What are the types of violence and insecurity that affect their ability to move about in public spaces? How are these negotiated? (Prompts: Do you carry something for protection, avoid certain areas, travel with companions, or ask for help?)
3. What kind of actions (policy, design, changes in men and boys' behavior) have been undertaken by different authorities toward this, and what have been their impact?
4. How safe is the connectivity and access to this public space?
5. What has influenced your views about this public space such as your own experiences, others' experiences, media reports, and stories? Share some concrete experiences or stories of safety in public spaces.
6. What are the three most important safety issues concerning this public space and why is that so?
7. How can we create friendly and inviting public spaces for gender minorities?

Open-ended questions for organizations working on accessibility, disability rights, and advocacy

1. What are the barriers to accessing public open spaces in the city, and what are the gendered aspects of disabilities?
2. What kind of actions (policy, design, awareness) have been undertaken by different authorities toward improving accessibility, and what has been their impact?
3. How accessible is this public space and is there any pre-planned information available about it?
4. What kind of amenities are available for persons with disabilities such as stepless walkways, public toilets, and sitting spaces?
5. What needs to be considered for people with reduced mobility, hearing impairment, and visual impairments?
6. What kind of grievance redress mechanisms are required to assist persons with disabilities?
7. How can service providers and co-users be sensitized on disability issues?

General Information

Name

Gender
- ☐ Female
- ☐ Male
- ☐ Other genders
- ☐ Prefer not to say

Profession

Designation
- ☐ Junior
- ☐ Mid-level
- ☐ Leadership

Organization

Disability, if any
- ☐ Mobility
- ☐ Hearing
- ☐ Vision
- ☐ Cognitive

Location

Source: Authors.

Appendix 2-5: Key informant interview questionnaire

1. What are the effects of climate change in this city/district?
2. How many genders are there in Bangladesh? What does gender equality mean to you?
3. What is the status of women, girls, gender minorities in this city/district (including access to public open spaces)? How has climate change exacerbated or ameliorated this?
4. What are the key public open spaces in this city, and how are they maintained? What makes these attractive to people, especially women, girls, persons with disabilities?
5. How is this public open space affected by disasters and climate change? What kind of water retention and drainage systems are in the public open space?
6. What are the key barriers that withhold women, girls, other genders and persons with disabilities from accessing and using this public open space?
7. How can we include women, girls, adolescents, elderly, and persons with disabilities meaningfully in the decision-making process of public space development?
8. What are the most important facilities for a public space to become safe, secure, and gender-equitable?
9. Does the public open space use any energy-efficient elements/ systems?
10. How is the public open space maintained?

General information

Name
Age
Gender
- ☐ Female
- ☐ Male
- ☐ Other genders
- ☐ Prefer not to say

Profession

Designation
- ☐ Junior
- ☐ Mid-level
- ☐ Leadership

Organization
Disability, if any
- ☐ Mobility
- ☐ Hearing
- ☐ Vision
- ☐ Cognitive

Location

Source: Authors.

Appendix 2-6: Occasional, rare, or non-user survey

1. Are you aware of the public open spaces in the vicinity? If yes, which are these?
2. Which factors influence your choice to visit or use this public open space? (Prompt: Perception and experience of safety, sexual abuse and harassment)
3. How do you feel about this public space?
   - ☐ Strongly negative
   - ☐ Somewhat negative
   - ☐ Somewhat positive
   - ☐ Strongly positive
4. Have you faced sexual abuse and harassment in the public open space in the last 6 months?
   - ☐ Yes
   - ☐ No
5. If yes, what type of sexual abuse and harassment did you face?
   - ☐ Staring
   - ☐ Eve teasing
   - ☐ Stalking
   - ☐ Groping
   - ☐ Others
6. How did you address it?
   - ☐ Ignored it and moved away
   - ☐ Accosted the perpetrator
   - ☐ Requested help from other users

continued on next page

Appendix 2-6 *continued*

☐ Reported it to the police
☐ Others

7. How has it affected your experience and access to the public open space?

    ☐ It has not affected my access
    ☐ I visit less often
    ☐ I come here with a male companion
    ☐ I come here with a female companion
    ☐ Others

8. Which three words would you use to describe this public open space?

    _____

9. Which two things would you like to do in this public space that you cannot do now?

    _____

10. What are the sounds that you associate with this public open space?

    _____

11. What are the smells or fragrances that you associate with this public open space?

    _____

General Information

Name

Gender
☐ Female
☐ Male
☐ Other genders
☐ Prefer not to say

Profession

Designation
☐ Junior
☐ Mid-level
☐ Leadership

Organization

Education
☐ Pursuing
☐ Completed
☐ Not applicable
☐ No schooling
☐ Primary
☐ Secondary
☐ University degree
☐ Postgraduate

Economic activity (and workstation, if applicable)
☐ Unemployed
☐ Part-time employment
☐ Full-time employment
☐ Retired
☐ Actively looking for a job

Household/ Family status
☐ Married
☐ Divorced
☐ Separated
☐ Widowed
☐ Single

Disability, if any (Select all that apply)
☐ Mobility
☐ Hearing
☐ Vision
☐ Cognitive
☐ Others

Number of dependents

Do you have a caregiver?
• Yes
• No

If yes,
☐ Part-time
☐ Full-time

Source: Authors.

Appendix 2-7: Age and gender counts

If there are entry/exit gates, then a surveyor can be located at each one. For smaller public open spaces, the surveyor can walk through the public open space at 15-minute intervals.

Time zone	Time	Children		Youth		Elderly		Persons with disabilities		Women	Men	Other genders
		G	B	G	B	W	M	W	M			

B = boys, G = girls, M = men, W = women.
Note: Time zone such as early morning, morning, afternoon, evening, night; Time: 15-minute intervals in 1 hour
Source: Authors.

Appendix 2-8: Checklist for assessing connectivity, access, amenities, safety, and security

SNo	Parameters	
A	**Connectivity and Accessibility**	
1	Is there a public transport stop within 400 meters (m) walking distance of the public open space?	• Yes • No
2	What is the mode of public transport? *Select all that apply*	• Bus • Train • Cycle rickshaw • Easy bike • Shared auto • Others
3	What is the average headway in the peak hours?	• <5 minutes • 5–10 minutes • 10–15 minutes • >15 minutes
4	What is the average headway in the off-peak hours?	• <10 minutes • 10–20 minutes • 20–30 minutes • > 30 minutes
5	Does the public transport stop include the following? *Indicate with a tick or a cross and provide notes*	• Consistent, well-maintained, and sufficient footpath access • Sufficient protection from the sun and rain • Uniformly well-lit • Clear line of sight and visibility • Sufficient seating during peak hours • Route map • Schedules and the estimated time of arrival • Real-time information
6	Does the access to the closest public transport stop include the following? *Indicate with a tick or a cross and provide notes*	• Gradual access ramps • Continuous and safe placement of tactile pavers providing a safe path • Audio announcements on public transport arrival are provided • Adequate, well-maintained signage and information for persons with visual and hearing impairments
7	Are the parking facilities for private vehicles priced based on demand and managed?	• Is there an on-street or off-street parking space within 400 m walking distance?

SNo	Parameters	
A	**Connectivity and Accessibility**	
		• Is the parking safe and accessible with consistent and well-maintained access paths and lighting? Is the on-street/off-street parking priced and managed? • Is there adequate and inclusive signage? • Are there enough parking spaces for persons with disabilities?
8	Are there parking facilities for bicycles?	• Is the on-street parking space safe and accessible with consistent and well-maintained access paths and lighting? • Is there adequate and inclusive signage?
9	Are the pedestrian, cycling infrastructure, and crossings safe?	• Are there well-lit, consistent, continuous, and wide footpaths? • Are the footpaths, clean and well maintained with no fixed or temporary obstructions? • Are there ramps where required with appropriate width and slope for persons on wheelchairs? • Do the footpaths have adequate tactile paving? • For roads below 24 m, are the street traffic calmed below 30 kilometers per hour (kph)? • For roads above 24 m, are there segregated, levelled, continuous, cycle tracks? • Are the intersections and crossings safe, accessible with refuge for pedestrians and cyclists?
B	**Spatial Layout**	
1	How do different socioeconomic groups use the public open space? • What kind of activities do different groups engage in? • Are there dominant groups? If yes, how so?	• Infants, toddlers and caregivers • Boys and girls (5–10 years) • Adolescent boys and girls (10–19 years) • Adult men and women: Consider young adults and older adults

continued on next page

Appendix 2-8 continued

SNo	Parameters	
B	**Spatial Layout**	
	Are certain groups underrepresented, spend less time? Photo document and sketch activities and make extensive notes.	• Pregnant women • Elderly men and women • Men and women with disabilities • Male and female livelihood workers • Gender minorities
2	What are the opportunities to increase their level and type of activity and encourage diverse users?	
C	**Amenities and Street Furniture**	
1	Which facilities and amenities are in the public open space and are they safe and accessible? *Describe these to illustrate the issues and improvements required* N.B. *Private nursing spaces and public toilets: If not in the public open space, is it available within a 200 m walking distance*	Facilities • Pedestrian-scale lighting • Seating • Drinking water facilities • Waste bins segregating dry and wet waste • Sheltered bicycle parking Amenities • Sheltered, enclosed nursing spaces • Gender-segregated, clean and well-maintained toilets with lighting, ventilation, water, soap, sanitary pad dispensing machines, separate dustbins for menstrual pads, hooks behind doors. • Universally accessible, gender-neutral public toilets with commodes for an adult and child, diaper changing station • Universally accessible signage and information
D	**Environment and Heritage**	
1	Is the public open space well shaded? *Describe these to illustrate the issues and improvements required*	• Yes • No • Partially
2	Does the public open space use any energy-efficient elements/systems?	Briefly document any elements that aim to conserve energy
3	How is the social, cultural, and built history addressed?	Briefly document the relevance of environmental, social, and cultural history, and any approaches adopted

SNo	Parameters	
D	**Environment and Heritage**	
4	What are the different types of vegetation and how do they protect the public open space from climate risks?	Photograph the trees, shrubs, plants, assess the wild variants and species; assess how it is connected or disconnected to existing water networks.
E	**Safety and Security**	
1	Visual connectivity *Describe these to illustrate the issues and improvements required*	• Are there clear lines of sight, without blind spots and dark corners? • Are park edges visually permeable?
2	Lighting	• Is there adequate lighting in the night?
3	Activity *Describe these to illustrate the issues and improvements required*	• Is the space active with a diverse mix of users? • Are there groups of men engaged in drinking and other unsafe practices?
4	Security guards	• Are there security guards to monitor the public open space?
5	Signage, information	• Is there information on existing helpline numbers? • Does the signage, advertising language communicate positive gender norms and socialization?

Source: Authors.

Appendix 2-9: Safety audits

Introduction for the safety audit

- Familiarize the participants with the process of planning and conducting the audits.
- Recommend involving stakeholders who have been living in the area for at least 1 year for an in-depth understanding.
- Share the map and the table with the participants and encourage them during the walk to observe the public open space.

Source: Adapted from the consolidated best practices by UN-Habitat, 2008.

Safety Walk methodology

On arrival – ask for the following details of each participant.

- Introduction
    - Sex
    - Age group (10–19, 20–29, 30–39, 40–49, 50–59, 60+)
    - Educational status (no schooling, primary, secondary, university degree, postgraduate)
    - Economic activity (unemployed, part-time employment, full-time employment, informal sector, retired)
    - Household/family status (married, divorced/ separated/ widowed, single)

- The facilitator can introduce themselves and provide a brief introduction on the necessity and objective of the safety audit, as well as an overview of the process.

- Explain the confidentiality rules for the session.

Note for facilitator: Where a neighborhood or whole area is to be covered, a sheet should be prepared for each street or sub-area visited; number each street/area on the map and the accompanying report.

Safety audit walk questionnaire

Name of area:
Date:
Code for the person:
Time and day of the walk:

Issue	Questions	Provide details
First Impressions	Which three words best describe this public open space?	
Lighting	How well-lit is the public open space?	☐ Well-lit ☐ Poorly lit ☐ Unlit
	Does this make you feel safe/ unsafe? Why is that so?	☐ Well-maintained ☐ Poorly maintained ☐ Unmaintained
Maintenance	How maintained is the public open space?	☐ Well-maintained ☐ Poorly maintained ☐ Unmaintained
	Does the general state of maintenance of the area make you feel safe/ unsafe? Why is that so?	☐ Yes ☐ No ☐ Maybe
Walkability	Are the walkways wide, unobstructed, levelled with access ramps?	☐ Yes, most of the walkways are ☐ Few of the walkways are ☐ None of of the walkways
	Does this make you feel safe/unsafe?	☐ Yes ☐ No ☐ Maybe Reasons
Amenities	Are there well-maintained amenities such as seating, public restrooms, nursing spaces?	☐ Sufficient seating in active areas ☐ Public rest rooms for men, women, universally accessible gender-neutral cubicles ☐ Private nursing areas Required amenities
	Are any amenities required, and what are these?	
	Do you feel safe/unsafe using these amenities? Why?	☐ Yes ☐ No ☐ Maybe Reasons

continued on next page

Appendix 2-9 continued

Presence of people, busy areas and isolated spaces	Are there a lot of people using this public open space, or are there places where it is empty and secluded, and are there spaces where people can hide?	
	Does this make you feel safe/ unsafe? Why? For example: Are there particular groups of people hanging around who make you feel unsafe?	☐ Yes ☐ No ☐ Maybe Reasons
Signage	Is there sufficient signage?	☐ Directional signage ☐ Information on grievance redress mechanisms ☐ Location of key landmarks, public transport stops Notes
	Does this make you feel safe/unsafe? Why?	☐ Yes ☐ No ☐ Maybe
Surveillance	Is there any form of formal surveillance?	☐ Police presence ☐ Security guard ☐ CCTV cameras ☐ Others
	Is there any form of informal surveillance (such as street vendors)?	

Safety Walk Report Card

Action

Use the scorecard to gather views from participants at the end of the safety walk. Each participant should score their overall experience on the walk. If the report card is being used with less literate groups, the numerical scoring can be replaced by colored stickers.

Purpose

To give everyone in the safety walk an opportunity to score the area individually. Safety walk organizers can also collate responses to provide a numerical scoring of perceptions of safety and security in the area.

Key:

1 = Very unsafe
2 = Unsafe
3 = Not consistently safe
4 = Quite safe
5 = Very safe

Alternative key:

Red = Unsafe or very unsafe
Yellow = Not consistently safe
Green = Safe or very safe

Parameter					
Issue	Rate from 1–5				
Overall sense of safety in the areas	1	2	3	4	5
Lighting					
Maintenance					
Crowded areas					
Isolated spaces					
Signage					
Presence of people					
Informal/formal surveillance					

Source: Authors.

Appendix 2-10: Accessibility audits

Introduction for the accessibility audit

- Familiarize the participants with the entire process of planning, designing, implementation, reporting, and follow-up of the audits.
- Involve at least one sign language interpreter.
- Consider participants residing in the area for at least 1 year.
- Share the map and the table with the participants and encourage them to observe the public open space.

Accessibility audit methodology

On arrival – ask for the following details of each participant.

continued on next page

Appendix 2-10 *continued*

- Introduction
    - Sex
    - Age group (10–19, 20–29, 30–39, 40–49, 50+)
    - Educational status (no schooling, primary, secondary, university degree, postgraduate)
    - Economic activity (business owner, unemployed, part-time employment, full-time employment, retired)
    - Household/family status (married, divorced/separated/ widowed, single)
    - Impairment (motor, visual, hearing)
- The facilitator can introduce themselves and provide a brief introduction on the objective and process of the accessibility audit.
- Explain the confidentiality rules for the session.
- A video recording of the participants maneuvering the public space must be taken to understand issues in navigation.

Name of area: Date: Code for the person: Time and day of the walk:			Responses	
	Questions related to accessibility in public open spaces	Yes	No	Do not know
Persons with limited mobility (including pregnant women, elderly)	Are there designated accessible parking spaces close to the entry?			
	Is there clear, well-placed signage with inclusive symbols?			
	Is there a main entrance or at least one entrance that is accessible?			
	Where the approach is not levelled, are there ramps?			
	Is the ramp of comfortable width and slope?			
	Is the walkway free of obstructions and levelled?			
	Questions related to accessibility in public open spaces	Yes	No	Do not know
	Is there accessible and comfortable seating?			
	Are there accessible toilet(s) in the premises?			
	Are resting facilities provided at regular intervals?			
Persons with limited visibility	Is there clear, well-placed signage with braille or raised lettering, and disability access symbols?			
	Is there an audio communication system in the queuing system, ticket office, or information desk?			
	Do pathways have surface differentiation in the form of tactile guiding and warning pavers or visual contrast?			
	Is the walkway free of obstacles?			
	Are drop-off areas clearly demarcated?			
Persons with limited hearing	Is there a clear and legible visual communication system in the queuing system, ticket office, or information desk?			
	Is there clear, well-placed signage with information such as opening times, points of interest, and maps?			

Sources: Adapted from National Disability Authority. 2012. Accessibility Toolkit. National Disability Authority: Mencap. 2016. *Disability Inclusion Toolkit Enabling Inclusive Youth Work*. Youth Inclusion Hub Partners.

Appendix 2-11: Understand the barriers, aspirations, and expectations of diverse groups and envision the green public open space

SNo	Tool	Recommended Resources	Planned Activity	Days
1	On-site exhibition	Two A1 exhibition panels with display: One panel with the base map of the public open space, and the second with two A1 charts • Table with a book and pen • Post-its, stickers (different shapes, smileys, thumbs-up) • Sketch pens/ Markers • Six volunteers working in batches of three, for 4 hours each.	• The first panel can include a base map with thumbs-up and thumbs-down on how users feel about different parts of the public open space, along with post-its inviting people to share the barriers, aspirations, and expectations of the space. • The second panel can include two A1 charts, with the principles of public space design. • Users can be invited to prioritize the three critical principles through stickers and write their vision for this public open space.	• 2 days (weekday and a weekend day): The timings can be decided based on the use of the public open space • Ensure gender balance in the participants
2	Visioning workshop and design charrette	Projector, screen, laptop, at least three microphones Each table • Round table with 5–7 participants • Base map of A1 size • One dozen tracing paper of A1 size • One moderator and one rapporteur • Post-its, stickers (different shapes, smileys, thumbs-up) • Sketch pens/ Markers Exhibition panels • Two A1 exhibition panels with display: One person at each panel	• Introduction by a higher-level dignitary • Presentation on the existing situation analyses focusing on the use of the public open space, findings of the participatory audits, on-site exhibition and key informant, semi-structured interviews, barriers, aspirations, and expectations. • Participants can then move through an exhibition. • Participants then break out into smaller facilitated groups to design the public open space and present it to each other. • The session concludes with key takeaways and next steps.	• 1 day (up to 6 hours) with snacks, lunch and tea/coffee • Ensure representation of children, adolescents, elderly, and persons with disabilities • Ensure gender balance in representation

Source: Authors.

Appendix 3: Create

Appendix 3-1: Organizing an on-site exhibition and a visioning workshop and design charrette

SNo	Tool	Recommended Resources	Planned Activity	Days
1	On-site exhibition	<ul><li>Two A1 exhibition panels with a display board: One panel with the base map of the public open space, and the second with two A1 charts</li><li>Table with a book and pen</li><li>Post-its, stickers (different shapes, smileys, thumbs-up)</li><li>Sketch pens/ Markers</li><li>Six volunteers working in batches of three, for 4 hours each</li></ul>	<ul><li>The first panel can include a base map with thumbs-up and thumbs-down on how users feel about different parts of the public open space, along with post-its inviting people to share the barriers, aspirations, and expectations of the space.</li><li>The second panel can include two A1 charts, with the principles of public space design (outlined in Section 2).</li><li>Users can be invited to prioritize the three critical principles through stickers and write their vision for this public open space</li></ul>	<ul><li>2 days, including a weekday and a weekend day: The timings can be decided based on the use of the public open space</li><li>Ensure gender balance in the participants</li></ul>
2	Visioning workshop and design charrette	<ul><li>Round tables with 5–7 participants</li><li>Four A1 flip charts per table</li><li>Base map of A1 size</li><li>One dozen tracing paper of A1 size</li><li>Projector, screen, laptop, at least two microphones</li><li>One moderator and one rapporteur</li><li>Exhibition panels</li><li>Four A0 exhibition panels with a display board: Two panels with the base map of the public open space</li><li>Two panels with 2 A1 charts</li><li>Post-its, stickers (different shapes, smileys, thumbs-up)</li><li>Sketch pens/ Markers</li><li>Two persons on each panel</li></ul>	<ul><li>Introduction by a higher-level dignitary</li><li>Presentation on the existing situation analyses focusing on the use of the public open space, findings of the participatory audits, on-site exhibition and key informant, semi-structured interviews, barriers, aspirations, and expectations</li><li>Participants can then move through an exhibition with two panels engaging them in assessing the public open space and articulating their vision for it.</li><li>The participants then break out into smaller facilitated groups to design the public open space and present it to each other.</li><li>The session concludes with key takeaways and next steps</li></ul>	<ul><li>1 day (up to 6 hours) with lunch and tea/ coffee</li><li>Ensure representation of children, adolescents, elderly and persons with disabilities</li><li>Ensure gender balance in the participants</li></ul>

Source: Authors.

Appendix 3-2: Universal and gender-responsive design guidelines

Design Elements	Universal Design Considerations		
	Physical Disability	Visual Impairment	Hearing Impairment
Accessible parking	• One accessible parking bay per 50 bays • Bay size 3,600 millimeters (mm) (including 1,200 mm for wheelchair assistive devices circulation, like rollators, and others) x 5,000 mm • Bay is located within 30 m of accessible main entrances • Designated parking space for adapted scooters/ tricycles to be provided • Provision of the footpath (1,200 mm wide) behind car parking for wheelchair movement • Provision of curb ramps (1,800 mm wide) on the footpath behind the parking at appropriate places	• Provision of pelican signals for pedestrians especially those with blindness (recommended) • No landscapes features (like tree branches and other elements) in the walkway pose an obstruction to persons with vision impairments • Provision of pedestrian symbols along with disability symbols painted before the zebra crossing lines	
Footpaths, walkways, and crossings	• Continuous levelled surface with an uninterrupted walking zone of at least 1.8 m • No obstructions in the clear width of the walkway • Clear headroom of 2,100 mm (minimum) in the clear width	• Clear walking zone of 1.8 m x 2.1 m, with no overhead obstructions or projections • Height of the footpath to be not more than 150 mm • Provision of pelican signals for pedestrians • Provision of pedestrian symbols along with disability symbols painted before the crossings	
Entrance to a park, playground	• Provision of the pedestrian gate with a clear width of 900 mm	• Tactile guiding and warning pavers (at least 600 mm width) at all important locations and amenities • Contrasting color schemes and nosing for steps or plinth edges	
Seating areas	• Sheltered/ shaded resting place at short intervals • Seating with a height of 450 mm to 500 mm and a backrest and hand rest at 700 mm height	• Well-illuminated seating areas with a firm paved surface in a contrasting color	
Vending Machines	• Vending machines to be accessible from 500 mm • Vending display to be at a height of 900 mm to 1,200 mm • Accessible vending machines with adequate knee space should be preferred	• Tactile warning tiles to be at 300 mm	• Provision of audio signals in vending machines and acoustically sound environments

continued on next page

Appendix 3-2 *continued*

Design Elements	Universal Design Considerations		
	Physical Disability	Visual Impairment	Hearing Impairment
Green Areas	• Regular cleaning of leaf litter to be carried out from the walkway • Inclusive components, like play equipment for children with disabilities, senior citizen corner		
Public Toilets	• Unit with multiple choices of toilets (including Indian squat and European water closet [WC]-type fixtures) and provision of grab rail on the adjacent wall to WC between 450 mm to 500 mm • Minimum size of the cubicle to be 2.2 m x 2 m with sufficient maneuvering space inside the cubicle and minimum 900 mm clear door width • Grab rails at both sides of the cubicle (with 680 mm clear width) and height between 650 mm to 700 mm • Unisex/gender-neutral toilet (with diaper changing area and adequate accessories) / at least one unisex/gender-neutral accessible washroom on all floors with child-friendly sanitation fixtures • At least one step-free urinal and at least one urinal at low height with grab rails in male toilets • Wash basin at an accessible-height between 750 mm to 800 mm and Grab rails on either side of the wash basin • L- shaped grab rails on the adjacent wall to the water closet and folding bar on the transfer/open side of the water closet • Easy door-closing mechanisms (simple lever-type attachment) with double swing doors • Flushing arrangements, dispensers, and toilet paper to be mounted between 300 mm x 800 mm	• Ensure visibility of public toilets from a distance with signage as per standards • Panic alarm buttons and an alarm signal outside with a flash sign light for emergencies • Inclusive signs for public toilets (signs for female, male, gender-neutral, family, and baby feeding areas)	
Drinking Water	• Drinking facility basin at a height of 800 mm to 900 mm and 480 mm wide • Tap 100 mm above from the basin	• Provision of lever-type taps	
Ticket Counter	• Counters with a height to be 750 mm and rounded counter edges • Counter to extend 480 mm on the outside with clear knee space below it		

continued on next page

Appendix 3-2 *continued*

Design Elements	Universal Design Considerations		
	Physical Disability	Visual Impairment	Hearing Impairment
Ramps	• Kerb ramps or raised islands at crossings • Ramps with both side handrails of gradient min 1:12		
Tactile flooring and Safety rails	• Provision of smooth, non-slippery, and uniform surface material walkway for comfortable movement of wheelchairs/ strollers/ crutches, and others • Selection is to be done by considering the ease of maintenance (across lifecycles) and longevity • At least two rows of tactile warning tiles should be provided near obstacles and curb ramps. • Location of litter bins, lighting poles, and others away from the Tactile Guiding Path (TGSI) • Safety rails at two heights (760 mm and 900 mm high) at required places including landscape features, like water elements, and others • Warning tiles at 300 mm from the railing throughout the length		
Bollards	• General spacing of bollards to be 750 mm wide and one space 900 mm wide • Height 1,000 mm • Tactile Guiding Surface Indicators (TGSIs) in the center of the clear space between bollards • Warning tiles at 300 mm on both sides of the bollards • Visible bollards through a contrasting color material against the floor surface with light reflective indicators/surface • Use of vandalism-proof and high-durability materials		
Grating for stormwater drains	• Longer dimension to be perpendicular to the direction of travel • Edges of gratings to be well concealed in the floor masonry/ civil work	• Perforated or grooves in the grating with space less than 12 mm for safe mobility or crossover by people using sticks/canes/wheelchairs/strollers	

continued on next page

Appendix 3-2 *continued*

Design Elements	Universal Design Considerations		
	Physical Disability	Visual Impairment	Hearing Impairment
Wayfinding and accessible information	• Wayfinding and directions at appropriate places with appropriate: orientation, route decision, route monitoring, destination recognition • Building directional signage and bulletin board signs to be at 1,800 mm from the finished floor level • Wall-mounted signs to be placed between 900 mm to 1,800 mm • Emergency exits should be clearly marked and emergency evacuation maps to be displayed at legible locations • SOS features, such as medical emergency systems, facility wheelchairs, defibrillators, and others	• Signages for accessible parking at visible locations, a 1,000 mm x 1,000 mm signboard, provided at 2,100 mm to 2,500 mm clear height • Tactile, multilingual (especially local vernacular), and braille signage • Colors of the signage should be distinguishable and fonts to be legible • Audio-tactile floor maps and floor-wise directories to be provided on every floor	• Audiovisual signages at appropriate places
Information Display Board	• Height to vary from 900 mm to 1,800 mm • Warning signage for slopes, obstructions, and water bodies to be provided at visible locations		• Audiovisual, tactile, and multisensory formats of information dissemination should be encouraged

Source: Adapted from Mencap. 2016. *Disability Inclusion Toolkit Enabling Inclusive Youth Work*. Youth Inclusion Hub Partners.

Appendix 3-3: Design brief for Patuakhali–Barishal Road, Kuakata, Bangladesh

1. Introduction

This design brief outlines the process of implementing the guidelines and formulating conceptual strategies for the redesign of Barisal–Patuakhali Road in Kuakata. It is a tool for design management for the *pourashavas*.

2. Gender and social inclusion

It is important to collect and analyze gender- and social-inclusion-related data for a macro-level understanding of the place before finalizing a design. In Kuakata, criteria such as child marriage prevalence, political participation, and literacy rate show gender disparity. In the Rakhain community, 1.6% of the local population and their indigenous livelihoods options are increasingly at risk. At the micro level, a participatory action approach was applied to understand the gender and social inclusion situation in Kuakata, which includes surveys, interviews, safety and accessibility audits, visioning workshop, and stakeholder consultation meetings. The findings of these methodical tools and initiatives ultimately informed the detail of the design for the street in Kuakata.

3. Site context

The site is a road stretch (880 m) from the fish market to the Kuakata sea beach. It is part of the main access road of Kuakata town, connecting Patuakhali and Barisal (Figure A3.1).

4. Climate vulnerability

The Kuakata beach has been facing erosion due to tidal surges. The beach used to be shrouded with coconut, palm, and mangrove forests, which had been washed by the sea. The stones along the embankment are falling apart. The Water Development Board is repairing the embankment and aims to increase its height by an additional 6 feet. As a result, evictions have begun along the embankment. Sandbags and asbestos sheets are used on the beach as a coping mechanism against the rising tides (Figure A3.2).

Figure A3.1: Connectivity and Access Roads to Kuakata

Source: Asian Development Bank.

Figure A3.2: Concrete Embankment Installed Along Kuakata Beach to Combat Rising Tides

Source: Asian Development Bank.

5. Process

After a rigorous literature and policy review, an inventory of existing civil society and rights-based organizations was prepared (Figure A3.3). After reaching out to prominent local, national, and international organizations working in Kuakata and adjacent areas, several stakeholder consultations were organized both virtually and in person. Local organizations introduced end users and community participants who are crucial in an inclusive design-building process. Before the fieldwork, a pilot was conducted with the help of the local organizations and field assistants, which helped build rapport, finalize field plans, and ultimately to have a successful community engagement process that informed the public space design for Kuakata (Figure A3.4).

The multistakeholder visioning workshop provided insights into climate change impacts. These include erosion, increasing salinity, extreme weather conditions, sea level rise, and impacted wildlife and migratory birds.

Figure A3.4: Visioning Workshop with the Community in Kuakata

Source: Asian Development Bank.

6. Design principles

The design criteria are derived from the principles for creating climate-resilient and gender-responsive public open spaces for coastal towns in Bangladesh (Figure A3.5).

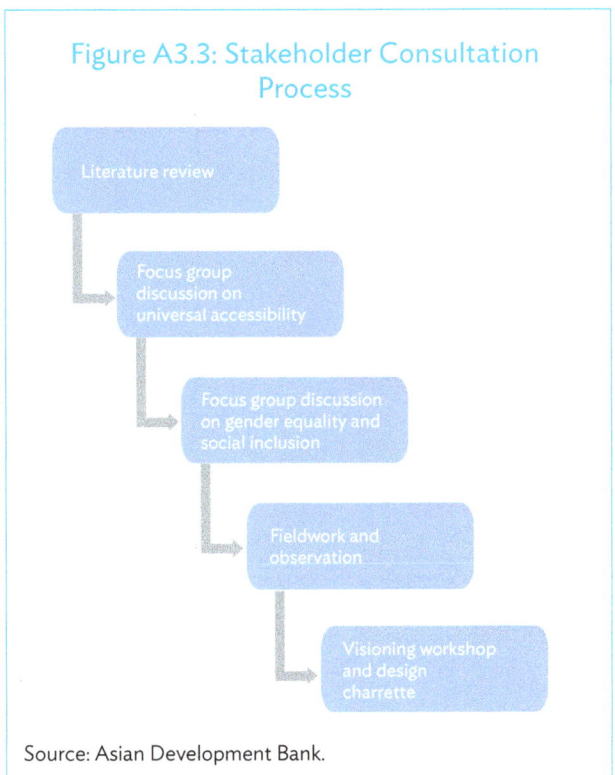

Figure A3.3: Stakeholder Consultation Process

Source: Asian Development Bank.

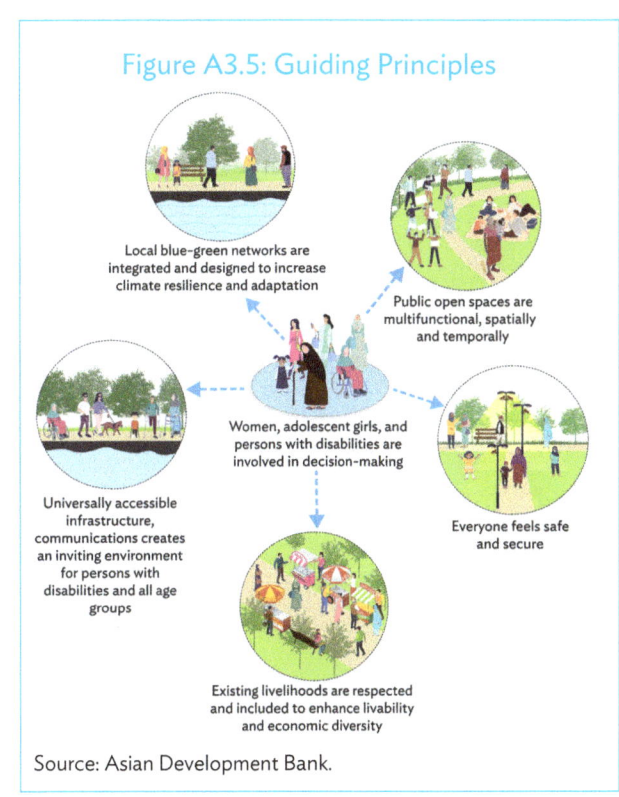

Figure A3.5: Guiding Principles

Source: Asian Development Bank.

7. Concept design

The concept sections are presented in the following figures to explain the subsequent details at different nodes. The right-of-way, landscaping, and drainage system will need to be assessed and validated (Figure A3.6 to Figure A3.9).

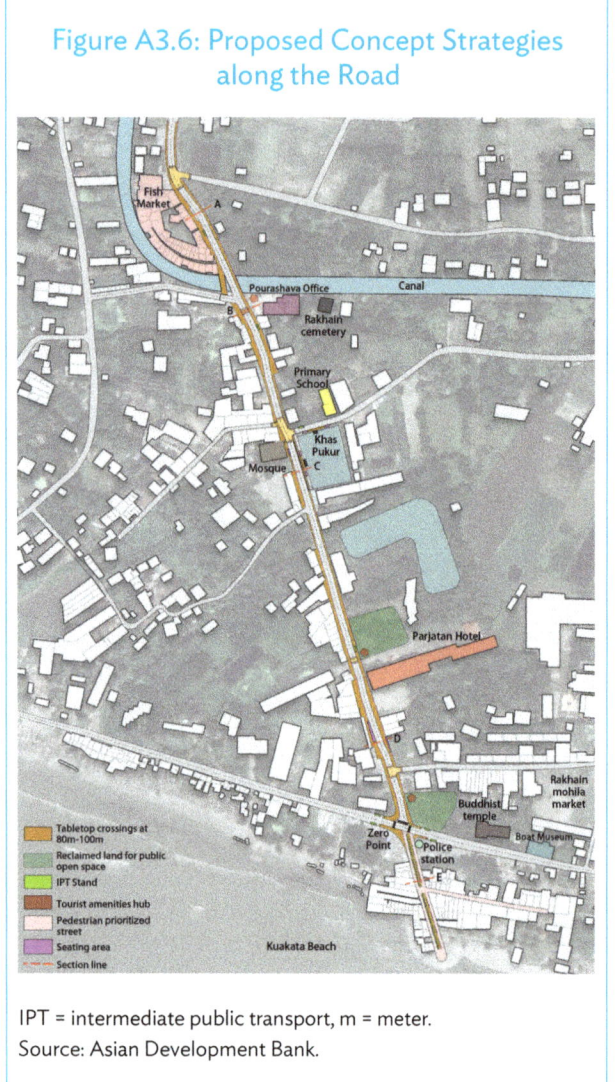

Figure A3.6: Proposed Concept Strategies along the Road

IPT = intermediate public transport, m = meter.
Source: Asian Development Bank.

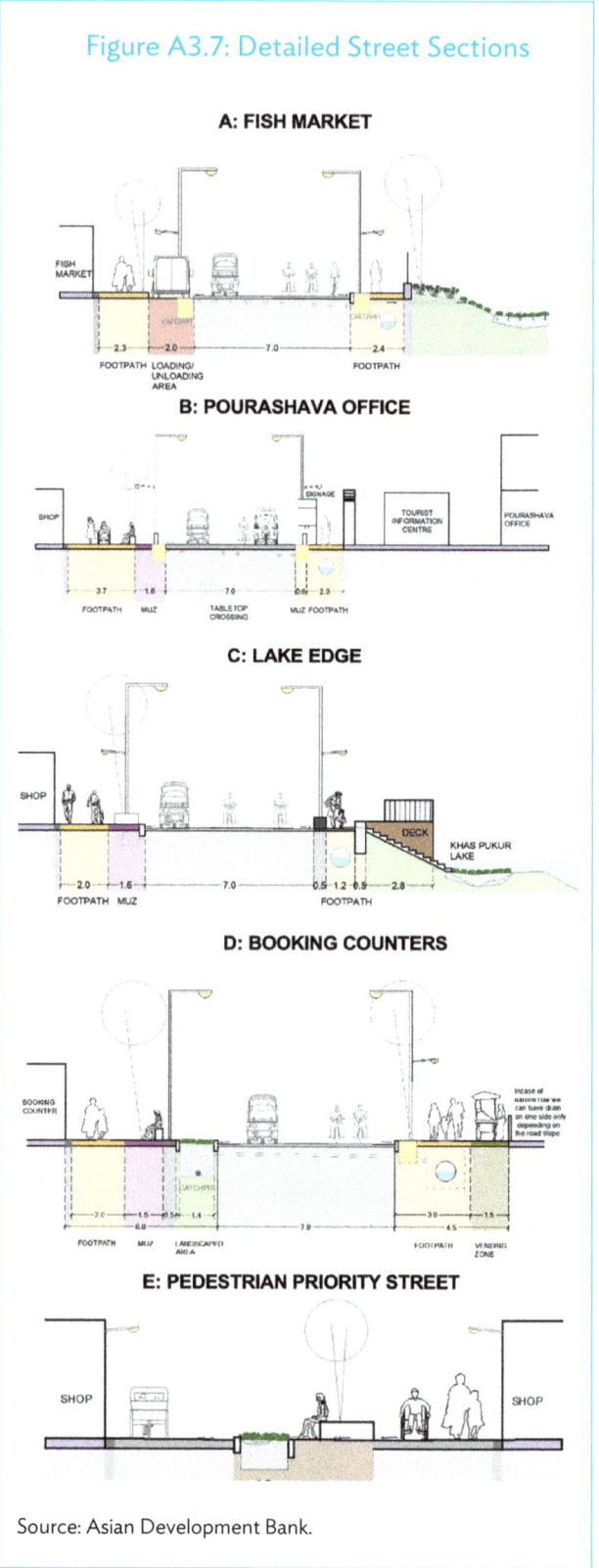

Figure A3.7: Detailed Street Sections

Source: Asian Development Bank.

Figure A3.8: Concept Design Near Booking Counters

Source: Asian Development Bank.

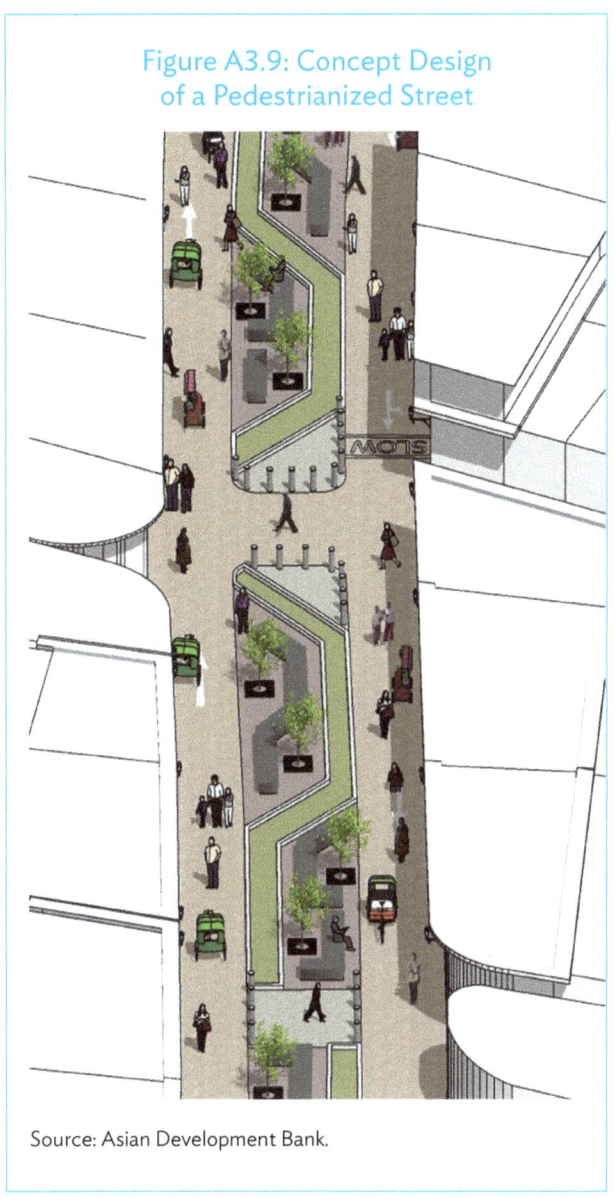

Figure A3.9: Concept Design of a Pedestrianized Street

Source: Asian Development Bank.

8. Amenities and street furniture

A matrix is created to provide guidance on the kind of amenities and facilities to be included in the hubs at specific locations (Table A3.1).

Table A3.1: Proposed Amenity Hubs at Different Locations

Location	Pourashavas Office	Bangladesh Parjatan Corporation	Water Development Board Land 1
Tourist information center			
Tourist police booth			
Public toilet			
Nursing station			
Drinking water			
Museum and oral history narratives about the Rakhain community			
Quiet, sheltered seating areas			
Quiet public open space for play			

Source: Authors.

9. Awareness and behavior-change strategies

- Strengthen the reporting and redressal system and increase awareness of the helpline numbers (Figure A3.10).
- Conduct annual gender-sensitization training for public service providers on language, conscious and unconscious gender bias, violence against women, and disability rights, with refresher sessions.
- Increase awareness of anti-sexual harassment laws and sensitize men and boys on women's and girls' experience of safety and sexual exploitation, abuse, and harassment.
- Increase awareness of positive role models to create friendly public open spaces for diverse gender communities.
- Update laws related to disability rights, and women's and girls' rights. Laws and policies need to be summarized and translated into Bangla in simple terms and distributed.

Figure A3.10: National Helpline Numbers

Sources: Bangladesh Police. 2020. Emergency Hotline Numbers. Bangladesh Police, Discipline Security Progress. 2020. (accessed 5 March 2023).

Appendix 3_4: Rupa Chaudhary Park, Bagerhat, Bangladesh

1. Introduction

The objective of this design brief for Bagerhat Pouro park is to equip the *pourashavas* in translating the conceptual strategies into detailed designs and implementation. These strategies are based on extensive on-site and offsite stakeholders' consultations. It is a tool for design management for the *pourashavas*.

2. Gender and social inclusion

It is important to collect and analyze gender and social-inclusion-related data for a macro-level understanding of the place before finalizing a design. In Bagerhat, criteria such as child marriage prevalence, employment, and literacy rate show gender disparity. At the micro level, a participatory action approach was applied to understand the gender and social inclusion situation in Bagerhat which includes surveys, interviews, safety and accessibility audits, visioning workshop, and stakeholder consultation meetings. The findings of these methodical tools and initiatives ultimately informed the detail of the design for the Pouro park in Bagerhat.

3. Site context

Rupa Choudhary Pouro Park is adjacent to the embankment road's longer side with a wide 8 feet wide footpath on the park's edge. The park has one main entrance toward the southwest side. The restaurant toward the southeast side is occupied by youngsters majorly during the evening times and has a continuous backdrop of dense vegetation covering the south and southeast edges of the park (Figure A3.11).

4. Climate vulnerability

The Pouro park site observes occasional water logging during the rainy season. A series of canals managed by sluice gates exists around the site to manage during heavy inundation. For a few months, cases of extreme heat are also observed. The park is a wide strip between an embankment road and a river with a larger length stretching north–south and a shorter side toward east–west. There is unavailability of natural shade.

5. Process

After a rigorous literature and policy review, an inventory of existing civil society and rights-based organizations was prepared. After reaching out to the prominent local, national, and international organizations working in Bagerhat, several stakeholder consultations were organized both virtually and in person (Figure A3.12).

Figure A3.11: Map of Rupa Chaudhary Pouro Park

Source: Asian Development Bank.

Figure A3.12: Stakeholder Consultation Process

Source: Asian Development Bank.

Local organizations introduced end users and community participants who are crucial in an inclusive design-building process. Before the fieldwork, a pilot was conducted with the help of the local organizations and field assistants, which helped to build rapport, finalize field plans, and ultimately to have a successful community engagement process that informed the public open space design for Bagerhat (photo).

Design Charrette and Visioning Workshop with the community in Bagerhat (photo by ADB).

6. Design principles

The design criteria are derived from the principles for creating climate-resilient and gender-responsive public open spaces for coastal towns in Bangladesh (Figure A3.13, Table A3.2).

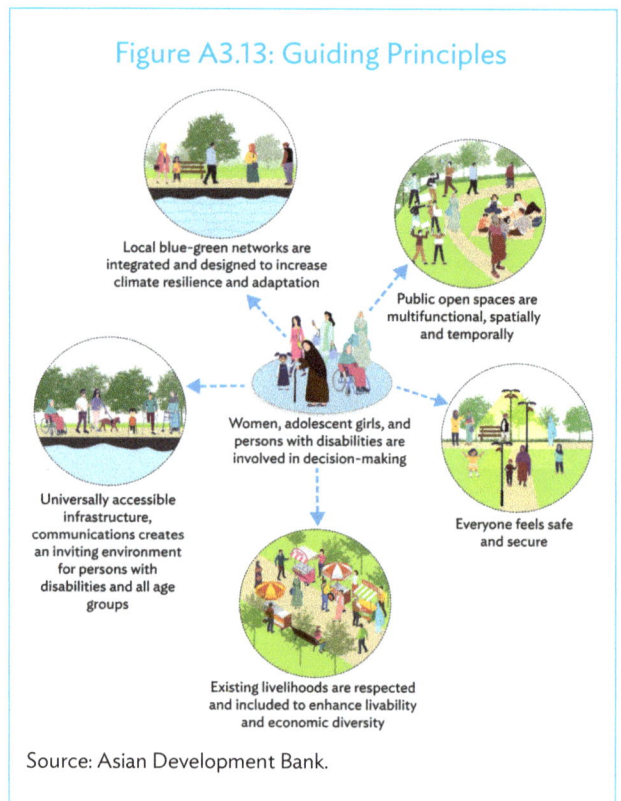

Figure A3.13: Guiding Principles

Source: Asian Development Bank.

Table A3.2: Design Elements for Rupa Chaudhary Pouro Park

SL	Broad Criteria	Design Elements
A	Inclusion	Amenities
	Women	Visual linkage
	Children	Universal access
	Senior residents and persons with disabiity	Children's play areas
	Poor community	Informal business facilities, paratransit stands, and cycle parking
B	Safety and Security	Visual linkage
		Lighting
		Define boundaries
		Zoning

continued on next page

Table A3.2 continued

SL	Broad Criteria	Design Elements
C	Climate resilence	Water management infrastructure
		Ground improvement and slope protection
		Landscaping
		Construction materials
D	Low maintenance	Elements exposed to weather and high-intensity use
		Element exposed to vandalism
		Network infrastructure; drainage system, electrical line, water supply
E	Optimum development	All amenities and infrastructure
F	Natural features	Site planning
		Management of hydrology
		Sightline and vista
		Land development and slope protection
G	Revenue generation	Rental rides
		Formal/informal business
		Improvement of the adjacent area
H	Integrating compatible functions in the park	Site planning
		Amenities and services
		Existing unused buildings and vacant land
I	Cultural/regional identity	Adjacent heritage sites
		Entrance
		Images
		Signage

Source: Authors.

7. Design

Based on the design principles, the concept plans and sections are prepared to explain the subsequent details proposed for the public open space (Figure A3.14).

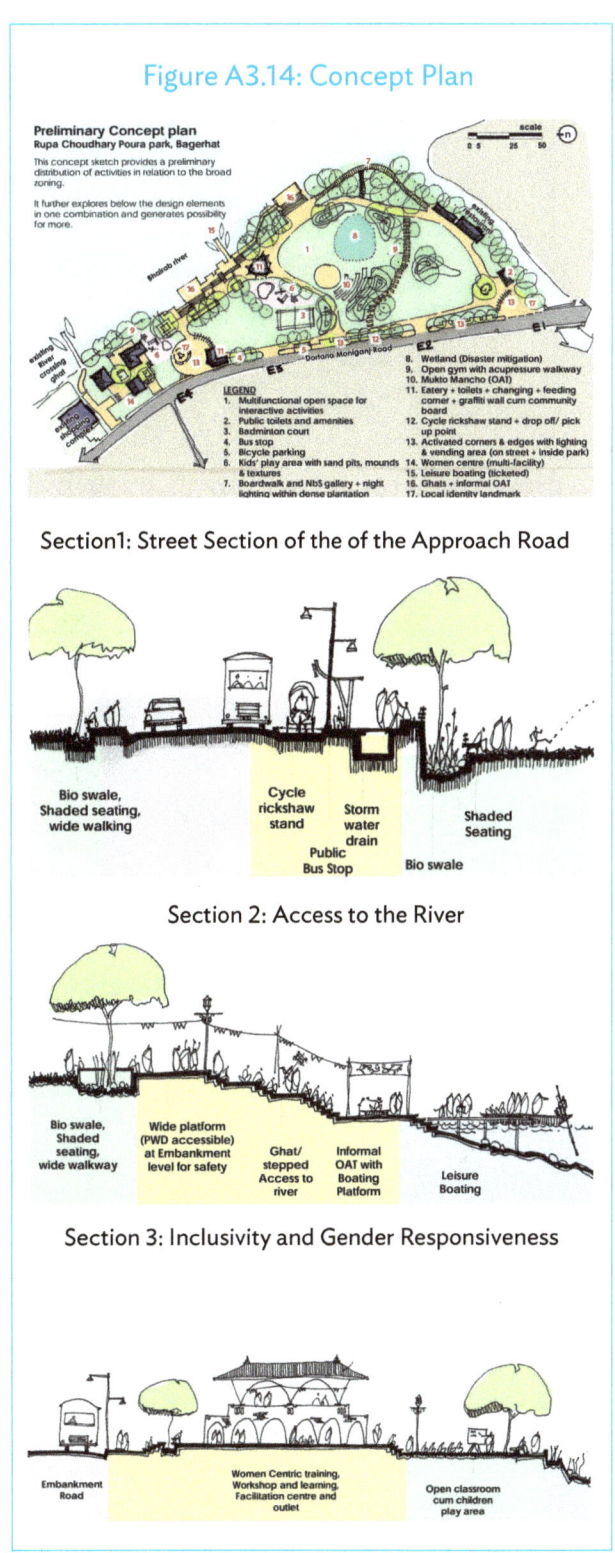

Figure A3.14: Concept Plan

Section1: Street Section of the of the Approach Road

Section 2: Access to the River

Section 3: Inclusivity and Gender Responsiveness

continued on next page

Figure A3.14 continued

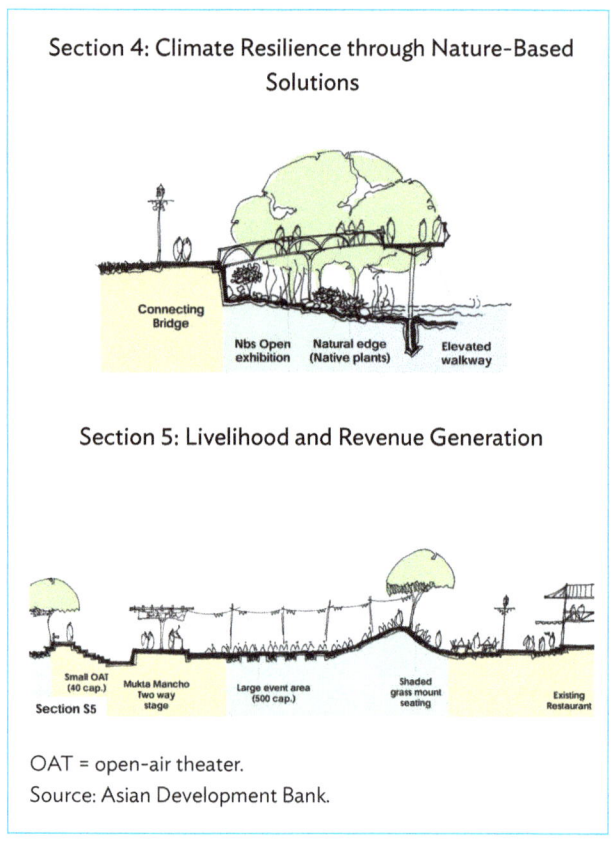

OAT = open-air theater.
Source: Asian Development Bank.

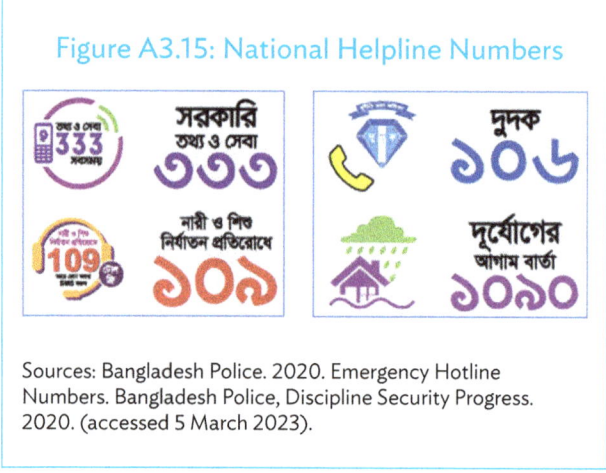

Figure A3.15: National Helpline Numbers

Sources: Bangladesh Police. 2020. Emergency Hotline Numbers. Bangladesh Police, Discipline Security Progress. 2020. (accessed 5 March 2023).

8. Awareness and behavior-change strategies

- Strengthen the reporting and redressal system and increase awareness of the helpline numbers (Figure A3.15).
- Conduct annual gender sensitization training for public service providers on language, conscious and unconscious gender bias, violence against women, and disability rights, with refresher sessions.
- Increase awareness of anti-sexual harassment laws and sensitize men and boys on women's and girls' experience of safety and sexual exploitation, abuse, and harassment.
- Increase awareness of positive role models to create friendly public open spaces for diverse gender communities.
- Updated laws related to disability rights, and women's and girls' rights. Laws and policies need to be summarized and translated into Bangla in simple terms and distributed.

Appendix 4: Manage

Maintenance schedule and considerations for the public open space

Street Furniture and Activities	Schedule	Key Considerations
Trash collection, cleaning, and litter removal	**Urgent**	• Collect trash from all the public dustbins, shops, public toilets, and related establishments. • Clean all the hardscapes including footpaths, bus stops, and other public areas. • Waste segregation, sorting, and recycling are recommended.
Streetlight and other electrical features	**Urgent**	• Pedestrian and traffic lights, garden lights, directional signage, and related electrical fittings. • Must detail specifications on the use of smart light-emitting diode (LED) lights with low energy consumption with sensors for power saving.
Public toilets	**Urgent**	• Clean multiple times a day. • Ensure availability of water, soap, tissues, and sanitary pads. • Repair any broken or malfunctioning fixtures.
Public elements and amenities	**Regular**	• Maintain and repair street furniture, trash bins, directional signage, fences, and water points.
Footpaths	**Regular**	• Repair and maintain footpaths, access ramps, paved surfaces, guiding, and warning pavers. • Additional monitoring to regulate encroachment, especially by parked vehicles.
Parking areas	**Regular**	• Maintain cleanliness, hygiene, and lighting in dedicated parking areas for bicycles, two-wheelers, and four-wheelers. • Ensure that waiting areas at the bus stop and bicycle parking are not encroached upon by personal vehicles. • Ensure that accessible parking spaces are not encroached on.
Natural vegetation	**Periodic**	• Clean tree pits, bioswales, medians, water absorption or percolation pits, and other planters and plantations. • Remove weed and trash. • Pest control. • Maintain irrigation system. • Prune trees and vegetation to ensure visibility. • Zero use of chemical fertilizers.
Water body and elements	**Periodic**	• Clean, desilt, and remove weed and garbage from water bodies. • Ensure that no wastewater is discharged in them, especially in water recharge or percolation infrastructure.
Urban form and activities	**Periodic**	• Maintain visual corridors and axes. • Position and sizes of advertisement panels • Monitor and prevent unauthorized construction of facilities operated by private agencies. • Any other obstructions that can compromise the public open space character.

Note: Urgent is daily, regular is at least twice a week, and periodic is at least twice a month.
Source: Authors.

Climate-resilient public open space. An open-air theater in Dhaka University, Bangladesh (photo by Sthanik Consultants, Lead Architects: Saiqa Iqbal Meghna and Suvro Sovon).

References

ACT. 2022. *Women's Safety Audit*. Government of the Australian Capital Territory, Community Services: https://www.communityservices.act.gov.au/women/womens_safety_audit.

Asian Development Bank (ADB). 2021. *Guidelines for Gender Mainstreaming Categories of ADB Projects*. https://www.adb.org/documents/guidelines-gender-mainstreaming-categories-adb-projects.

ADB. 2022a. *Coastal Towns Climate Resilience Project: Climate Risk and Adaptation Assessment*. People's Republic of Bangladesh. https://www.adb.org/sites/default/files/linked-documents/55201-001-ld-02.pdf.

ADB. 2022b. *Gender-Responsive Procurement in Asia and the Pacific: An Opportunity for an Equitable Economic Future*. ADB.

ADB and Tbilisi Municipality. 2021. *Fair Shared Green and Recreational Spaces: Guidelines for Gender-Responsive and Inclusive Design*. ADB. http://dx.doi.org/10.22617/TIM210525-2.

Bangladesh National Building Code (BNBC). 2015.

Bangladesh Police Discipline Security Progress. 2020. Emergency Hotline Numbers. https://www.police.gov.bd/ (accessed 5 March 2023).

Barcelona Field Studies Centre S.L. GCSE Coasts Vocabulary. https://geographyfieldwork.com/GeographyVocabularyGCSECoasts.htm.

Brown, G., P. Khan, and S. Hung. 2021. Gender-Responsive and Inclusive Urban Planning. In B. Susantono and R. Guild, eds. *Creating Livable Asian Cities*. ADB.

The Center for Rural Pennsylvania. 2010. *Planning for the Future: A Handbook on Community Visioning*. https://conservationtools.org/library_items/699.

CEO Water Mandate. 2014. *Driving Harmonization of Water-Related Terminology*. UN Global Impact. https://ceowatermandate.org/wp-content/uploads/2019/11/terminology.pdf

Conservation International. 2019. *A Practical Guide to Implementing Green-Gray Infrastructure*. https://initiative-mangroves-ffem.com/wp-content/uploads/2019/09/ggi_practicalguide_190807.pdf.

Consortium for DEWATS Dissemination (CDD). 2019. *Waterbody Rejuvenation - A Compendium of Case Studies*. Bengaluru. https://cddindia.org/wp-content/uploads/WBR-compendium-by-CDD.pdf#:~:text='Waterbody%20Rejuvenation%20%E2%80%93%20A%20Compendium%20of,take%20on%20the%20rejuvenation%20methodology.

Council of Europe. 2023. What is Gender-based Violence? https://www.coe.int/en/web/gender-matters/what-is-gender-based-violence.

Encyclopædia Britannica. Aquifer. https://www.britannica.com/science/aquifer.

Frances, R., M. Coughlan, and P. Cronin. 2009. Interviewing in Qualitative Research: The One-to-one Interview. *International Journal of Therapy and Rehabilitation*, 16 (6), pp. 309-314. doi:https://doi.org/10.12968/ijtr.2009.16.6.42433.

GIZ. 2020. *A Tactical Urbanism Guidebook*. New Delhi. https://www.transformative-mobility.org/assets/publications/TrainingMaterial_A_Tactical_Urbanism_Guidebook.pdf.

Governent of Australia, State Government of Victoria. 2016. *Urban Design Guidelines for Victoria*. https://www.urban-design-guidelines.planning.vic.gov.au/toolbox/glossary.

Government of Australia, State of Queensland, Queensland Reconstruction Authority. 2011–2022. Flood terms and Definitions. https://www.qra.qld.gov.au/resilience/flood-resilience/flood-terms-and-definitions.

Government of Bangladesh, Bangladesh Planning Commission, GED. 2020. *Bangladesh Delta Plan 2100*. National Economic Council. General Economics Division. https://bdp2100kp.gov.bd/Document/ReportPdfView.

Government of Bangladesh, Bangladesh Planning Commission, General Economics Division (GED). 2020. 8th Five Year Plan, July 2020–June 2025 : Promoting Prosperity and Fostering Inclusiveness. Dhaka, Bangladesh. https://www.prb.org/wp-content/uploads/2022/03/8th-Five-Year-Plan-compressed.pdf.

Government of Bangladesh, Ministry of Environment, Forest and Climate Change (MoEFCC). 2022. National Adaptation Plan of Bangladesh (2023–2050). https://www4.unfccc.int/sites/SubmissionsStaging/Documents/202211020942---National%20Adaptation%20Plan%20of%20Bangladesh%20(2023-2050).pdf.

Government of British Columbia. 2023. Wildfire Glossary. https://www2.gov.bc.ca/gov/content/safety/wildfire-status/about-bcws/glossary#W.

Government of California, Department of Water Resources. California Water Plan Glossary. https://water.ca.gov/Water-Basics/Glossary.

Government of the United States, CDCP. 2022. Adolescent and School Health. https://www.cdc.gov/healthyyouth/terminology/sexual-and-gender-identity-terms.htm.

Government of the United States, Centers for Disease Control and Prevention (CDCP). 2017. Natural Disasters and Severe Weather. https://www.cdc.gov/disasters/extremeheat/heat_guide.html.

Government of the United States, Department of Health and Human Services, State of Tennessee Department of Mental Health and Substance Abuse Services, Substance Abuse and Mental Health Services Administration (SAMSA). 2014. 2012 *Town Hall Meetings to Prevent Underage Drinking: Moving Communities Beyond Awareness to Action*. https://store.samhsa.gov/product/2012-Town-Hall-Meetings-to-Prevent-Underage-Drinking-Moving-Communities-Beyond-Awareness-to-Action/SMA14-4838.

Government of the United States, Department of Interior, Bureau of Land Management (BLM). 2003. Glossaries of BLM Surveying and Mapping Terms. https://www.blm.gov/or/gis/geoscience/files/BLMglossary.pdf.

References

Government of the United States, Sacramento County. Water Resources. Stormwater Quality Program: https://waterresources.saccounty.gov/stormwater/Pages/glossary.aspx.

Involve. 2018. Design Charrette. https://involve.org.uk/resources/methods?show=pager&page=0%2C2.

Istituto Nazionale di Urbanistica (INU). 2016. Charter of Public Space. Biennial of Public Space. https://inu.it/wp-content/uploads/Inglese_CHARTER_OF_PUBLIC_SPACE.pdf.

Jabeen, H. 2019. *Gendered Space and Climate Resilience in Informal Settlements in Khulna City, Bangladesh. Environment and Urbanization* 31 (1), pp. 115–138. doi:https://doi.org/10.1177/0956247819828274.

Mencap. 2016. *Disability Inclusion Toolkit Enabling Inclusive Youth Work.* Youth Inclusion Hub Partners. https://www.mencap.org.uk/sites/default/files/2016-06/TOOLKIT-NI.compressed.pdf.

Merriam-Webster. Bazaar (accessed 12 February 2023).https://www.merriam-webster.com/dictionary/bazaar.

Minnehaha Creek Watershed District (MCWD). 2019. Tree Trenches. https://www.minnehahacreek.org/education/keep-our-water-clean-our-communities/tree-trenches#:~:text=A%20tree%20trench%2C%20often%20known,of%20trees%20in%20urban%20areas.

National Association of City Transportation Officials (NACTO). 2013. *Urban Street Design Guide.* https://nacto.org/publication/urban-street-design-guide/street-design-elements/stormwater-management/bioswales/.

National Disability Authority. 2012. *Accessibility Toolkit.* https://nda.ie/publications/accessibility-toolkit.

NHC. 2012. National Helpline Centre for Violence against Women and Children. Department of Women Affairs : http://nhc.gov.bd/.

Oasis Designs Inc. 2012. Storm Water Management: Retrofitting Our Urban Streets for Sustainable Drainage. UTTIPEC. https://oasisdesigns.org/stormwater.pdf.

Project for Public Spaces (PPS). 2016. *Placemaking - What If We Build Our Cities around Places?* https://www.greenflagaward.org/resources-research/guidance/placemaking-what-if-we-build-our-citiies-around-places/.

PPS. 2007. What Is Placemaking? RProjects for Public Spaces: https://www.pps.org/article/what-is-placemaking.

Social Development Direct International (SDD). 2013. *Making Cities and Urban Spaces Safe for Women and Girls: Safety Audit Participatory Toolkit.* https://resourcecentre.savethechildren.net/document/making-cities-and-urban-spaces-safe-women-and-girls-safety-audit-participatory-toolkit/.

United Nations Department of Economic and Social Affairs (UNDESA). 2010. *Analysing and Measuring Social Inclusion in a Global Context.* New York. https://www.un.org/esa/socdev/publications/measuring-social-inclusion.pdf.

United Nations Entity for Gender Equality and the Empowerment of Women (UN Women). 2021. Accessibility Audit. https://www.unwomen.org/en/digital-library/publications/2021/07/brief-accessibility-audit.

United Nations Environment Programme (UNEP) Carribean Environment Programme (CEP). 1994. *Guidelines for Sediment Control Practices in the Insular Caribbean.* https://wedocs.unep.org/bitstream/handle/20.500.11822/28540/CEP_TR_32-en.pdf?sequence=1&isAllowed=y.

United Nations High Commissioner for Refugees (UNHCR). 2023. What Is Sexual Exploitation, Abuse and Harassment? https://www.unhcr.org/ie/what-we-do/how-we-work/tackling-sexual-exploitation-abuse-and-harassment/what-sexual-exploitation.

United Nations Human Settlements Programme (UN-Habitat). 2009. *Women's Safety Audits: What Works and Where?* UN-Habitat Safer Cities Programme. https://unhabitat.org/womens-safety-audit-what-works-and-where.

UN-Habitat. 2015. *Global Public Space Toolkit: From Global Principles to Local Policies and Practice.* https://unhabitat.org/global-public-space-toolkit-from-global-principles-to-local-policies-and-practice.

UN-Habitat. 2020a. City-Wide Public Space Strategies: A Guidebook for City Leaders. United Nations Human Settlements Programme. https://unhabitat.org/sites/default/files/2020/03/cwpss_guidebook_20200116.pdf.

UN-Habitat. 2020b. *Public Space Site-Specific Assessment: Guidelines to Achieve Quality Public Spaces at Neighbourhood Level.* UN-Habitat. https://unhabitat.org/public-space-site-specific-assessment-guidelines-to-achieve-quality-public-spaces-at-neighbourhood.

United Nations Office for Disaster Risk Reduction (UNDRR). Hazard. https://www.undrr.org/terminology/hazard.

UNDRR. Resilience. https://www.undrr.org/terminology/resilience.

United Nations Population Fund (UNFPA) and United Nations Children's Fund (UNICEF). 2021. Joint Evaluation of the UNFPA-UNICEF Joint Programme on the Elimination of Female Genital Mutilation: Accelerating Change Phase III (2018–2021). https://www.unfpa.org/sites/default/files/admin-resource/thematic%20note%201_gender_final.pdf.

UNICEF. 2020. *Advancing Positive Gender Norms and Socialization through UNICEF Programmes: Monitoring and Documenting Change.*

United States Army Corps of Engineers (USACE). 2003. *Coastal Engineering Manual.* https://www.publications.usace.army.mil/Portals/76/Publications/EngineerManuals/EM_1110-2-1100_App_A.pdf.

University of California, Los Angeles (UCLA) Center for Health Policy Research. 2005. Health DATA Program – Data, Advocacy and Technical Assistance. Health DATA. https://healthpolicy.ucla.edu/programs/health-data/trainings/Pages/community-assessment.aspx.

Women with Disabilities Development Foundation (WDDF). 2014. *Persons with Disabilities Rights And Protection Act 2013 User-Friendly Booklet.* Bangladesh. https://www.ilo.org/dyn/natlex/docs/ELECTRONIC/95795/118013/F51789448/BGD95795%20Booklet.pdf.

Work for a Better Bangladesh (WBB). 2015. Parks and Playgrounds in Dhaka: Taking Stock and Moving Forward. http://www.wbbtrust.org/view/research_publication/71.

World Health Organization (WHO). Gender. https://www.who.int/health-topics/gender#tab=tab_1.

WHO. Floods. https://www.who.int/health-topics/floods#tab=tab_1.

www.ingramcontent.com/pod-product-compliance
Lightning Source LLC
Chambersburg PA
CBHW040930240426
43667CB00027B/2999